Complete
Handyman
do-it-yourself
Encyclopedia

do-it-

- ► Home Modernizing
- ► Home Repair and Improvement
- ► Auto Repair and Maintenance
- ► Appliance Repair
- ► Furniture Building
- ► Interior Home Projects
- ► Exterior Craft Projects
- ► Gardening
- ► Use of Hand and Power Tools
- ► Boat Building
- ► Boat Handling
- ► Fishing and Fishing Equipment
- ► Hunting and Hunting Equipment
- ► Camping and Camping Equipment
- ► Hobbies and Crafts
- ► Radio, TV and Electronics
- ► Electrical Installation

Complete
Handyman
yourself
Encyclopedia

A COMPILATION OF SPECIAL INTEREST PROJECTS AND
MANUALS FOR THE REPAIR AND CARE OF HOMES,
AUTOS, APPLIANCES, HOBBY EQUIPMENT.

by the editors of

Science &
Mechanics

16
SCREENS
SPARK PLUG

H. S. STUTTMAN CO., INC. *publishers*   New York, N.Y. 10016

PRINTED IN THE UNITED STATES OF AMERICA

6P-2861-35(211)

VOLUME 16

How to Make Your Own Window Screens

These durable screens will last for many seasons yet are relatively easy to construct

▲ Strips rabbeted from screen stock before assembly hold screening firmly over frame when they are nailed back in place to serve as molding. Nailing action forces wire to follow angled shape of the strips, pulling it tight.

IF NEW SCREENS ARE needed and you have access to a power saw, here is a simple, yet efficient, way to build durable frames that will give years of trouble-free service.

There isn't a tack in the design, yet you'll have to break the wire cloth before it will pull out from any rail or stile. Ordinary screen stock is used throughout for all framing and strips, and a quickly-rigged corner jig assures strong and accurate joints. Select a fiberglass screening for its reflection-free, no-stretch properties.

Measure your window openings at outside edge of the screen stops, then deduct ⅛-inch from height and width for actual screen sizes. For each window, order screening within ½-inch of height and width, enough standard screen stock to cut out the top and bottom rails, eight to ten #10 x 2-inch flat head brass screws (depending whether center rail is used or not), and an 8-inch length of ½-inch doweling. For every three screens which will have a narrow center rail, add width of this rail to your screen stock order. A ½-pound box of copper or aluminum nails ¾- to 1-inch long and a quart of paint will be sufficient for the average job.

Begin framing by cutting the screen stock as shown in the drawing, making all stiles full length and rails 1¼-inch narrower than actual screen width. Now set your saw table to cut a 60° angle rabbet along inside top edge of all the pieces, as shown in the drawing. Be sure to use a narrow blade and save the cut-out strips for later use as molding.

Cut notches in the stiles for the end rails, also for any center rail, which should always be aligned with the meeting rail of its window.

For an easy way to make strong corner joints, clamp frame members to a square panel cut from plywood scrap as shown in the drawing. Doing one corner at a time, drill an end rail for ½-inch doweling and a stile for #10 screws as shown in the drawing. Install dowel and fasten with 2-inch screws. The dowel will keep the long screws from pulling out of the end grain, making a much stronger joint. Install a center rail

CUT FIBER GLASS SCREENING SAME SIZE AS FRAME

SCREEN SPLINE

MITER

$\frac{1}{8}$" LESS THAN WTH. OF OPENING

$\frac{1}{8}$" LESS THAN HT OF OPENING

$\frac{3}{4}$ TO 1" NAILS

2$\frac{1}{2}$ TO 3"

#10 X 2" F.H. BRASS SCREW

CENTER RAIL AT HEIGHT OF WINDOW MEETING RAIL

END RAILS (CUT 2$\frac{1}{4}$" LESS THAN FULL WIDTH)

$\frac{5}{8}$ X 1$\frac{3}{4}$" NOTCH

STILES (CUT FULL LG.)

FRAMING

STILE

$\frac{1}{2}$" DOWEL

$\frac{5}{8}$"

$\frac{3}{16}$" DRILL, C'SINK FOR #10 X 2" F.H. BRASS SCREW

END RAIL

CORNER JOINT

SCREEN MOLDING

$\frac{1}{8}$" $\frac{5}{8}$"

$\frac{3}{8}$"

1$\frac{1}{8}$"

60°

SECTION A-A

1$\frac{3}{4}$"

$\frac{1}{2}$" DOWEL

SCRAP

SQUARE PLYWOOD CORNER

CORNER JIG

CHISEL AWAY TIP OF SCREEN LEDGE TO TAKE SPLINE

SCREEN LEDGE

after outside frame is finished, one screw at each joint.

Cut out any protruding wood on the rabbeted edges with a chisel, then replace the strips temporarily to mortise the ends. At this point, sand all framing and outside surfaces of the strips. Then paint them to suit your home exterior.

Now lay screening over a frame, line up a wire strand with inner edge of a stile, and replace the strip previously rabbeted from this edge. Beginning at the center and working toward ends, nail strip through wire into frame as in the drawing. Repeat the process with an adjoining strip. Nail up remaining strips after pulling screening taut.

When all moldings are in place, cut away excess screening on outside edge of the molding with a razor blade or utility knife. Dot the nail heads with matching paint, and your screen is ready for the window hardware and installation.   D.M.S.

See also: ALUMINUM; BREEZEWAYS; STORM DOORS AND WINDOWS.

▲ *Finished screen, ready to install.*

◀ *Saw table set to cut the acute-angled rabbet in edge of screen stock with a 1/16-inch ply tooth circular blade.*

How to Get Started Snorkeling or Scuba Diving

Almost anyone who knows how to swim can enjoy either of these exciting water sports

BECOMING A SCUBA DIVER today requires about 28 to 40 hours of your time for professional instruction in a pool, open water and classroom. It also requires minimal equipment expense, equal to the price of a "top-of-the-line" set of golf clubs.

Scuba diving lessons are available at scuba clubs, YMCAs, adult education courses and some resort hotels, as well as through sporting goods dealers.

Instructors generally hold one or several cards from any number of national groups, stating that they are officially qualified to teach diving, or more precisely, diving with scuba, which is an acronym for Self Contained Underwater Breathing Apparatus.

Major agencies certifying diving competence in both instructors and the students they teach include National Association of Underwater Instructors (NAUI); Professional Association of Diving Instructors (PADI); National Association of Skin Diving Schools (NASDS); Scuba Schools International (SSI); plus the YMCA.

Upon successful completion of diver training, it's critical that you receive a certification card from one of the above associations because some diving gear shops may refuse to sell you air if you don't have it. And without air you simply can't dive.

Normally, an applicant starting in a scuba class needs only fins, mask and snorkel.

The first few lessons will cover the physiology of diving, primarily the effects of increased pressure on various parts of the human body. They'll also help a student become proficient first in using the raw tools of skin diving. These are basic "aids" to diving and include no scuba gear at all; only fins, mask and snorkel.

Fins accelerate a swimmer through the water much faster than is possible with only bare feet. A mask provides clear underwater vision, creating an air pocket between the face plate and the eyes. Lacking this air space, a diver would be virtually blind in water. In addition, a mask protects the eyes from irritations caused by prolonged direct contact with salt and other minerals in water. The snorkel enables

Spearfishing

THE SPEARGUN

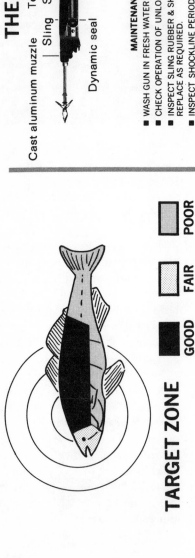

Cast aluminum muzzle

Sling

Spacing tube

Tempered stainless steel shaft

Hardened sear

Dynamic seal

Dynamic seal

Dynamic seal

MAINTENANCE SUGGESTIONS

- WASH GUN IN FRESH WATER AFTER USE.
- CHECK OPERATION OF UNLOADED GUN BEFORE USE – SAFETY – TRIGGER.
- INSPECT SLING RUBBER & SHOCK ABSORBER FOR WEAR OR DAMAGE – REPLACE AS REQUIRED.
- INSPECT SHOCKLINE PERIODICALLY.
- PERIODICALLY INSPECT SPEARHEAD – TIGHTEN ON SHAFT.

TARGET ZONE

■ GOOD
▨ FAIR
▧ POOR

SAFETY RULES

- NEVER LOAD OR SHOOT A SPEARGUN OUTSIDE OF WATER.
- KEEP YOUR SPEARGUN ON SAFETY UNTIL READY TO AIM.
- INSURE IDENTITY OF YOUR GAME BEFORE AIMING.
- UNLOAD YOUR SPEARGUN BEFORE LEAVING THE WATER.
- USE A FLOTATION DEVICE TO HOLD GAME AND PROVIDE RESTING PLATFORM.
- BIG GAME REQUIRES SPECIAL TECHNIQUES. ASK YOUR INSTRUCTOR FOR ADVICE.
- AVOID CARRYING GAME ON YOUR PERSON WHILE IN THE WATER.

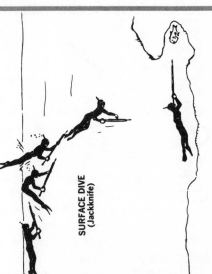

SURFACE DIVE
(Jackknife)

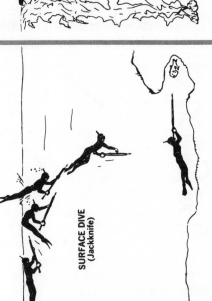

VERTICAL DIVE
– FEET FOREMOST–
(Kelp Dive)

The Snorkel

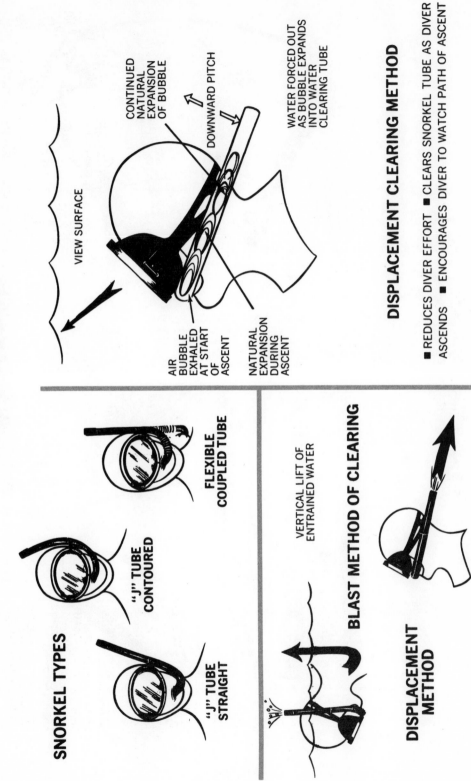

SNORKEL TYPES

"J" TUBE STRAIGHT

"J" TUBE CONTOURED

FLEXIBLE COUPLED TUBE

VIEW SURFACE

CONTINUED NATURAL EXPANSION OF BUBBLE

DOWNWARD PITCH

WATER FORCED OUT AS BUBBLE EXPANDS INTO WATER CLEARING TUBE

AIR BUBBLE EXHALED AT START OF ASCENT

NATURAL EXPANSION DURING ASCENT

DISPLACEMENT CLEARING METHOD

- REDUCES DIVER EFFORT ■ CLEARS SNORKEL TUBE AS DIVER ASCENDS ■ ENCOURAGES DIVER TO WATCH PATH OF ASCENT

VERTICAL LIFT OF ENTRAINED WATER

BLAST METHOD OF CLEARING

DISPLACEMENT METHOD

Swim Fin Propulsion

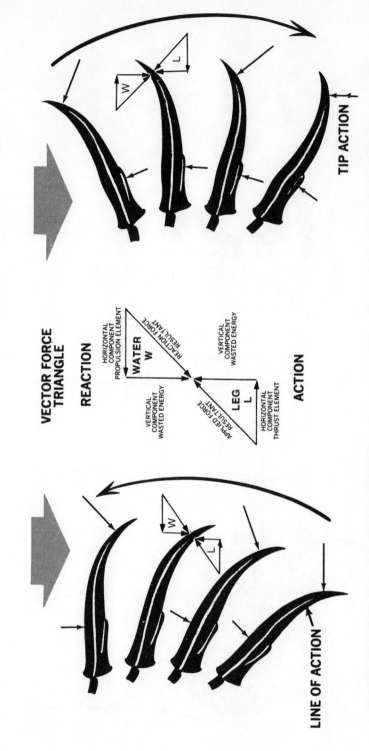

TIP ACTION

VECTOR FORCE
TRIANGLE

REACTION

HORIZONTAL
COMPONENT
PROPULSION ELEMENT

WATER
W

REACTION FORCE
RESULTANT

VERTICAL
COMPONENT
WASTED ENERGY

VERTICAL
COMPONENT
WASTED ENERGY

APPLIED FORCE
RESULTANT

LEG
L

HORIZONTAL
COMPONENT
THRUST ELEMENT

ACTION

LINE OF ACTION

FIN PROPULSION IS A PRACTICAL APPLICATION OF NEWTON'S THIRD LAW OF MOTION "EVERY ACTION IS OPPOSED BY AN EQUAL AND OPPOSITE REACTION." LEG AND ANKLE MUSCLES VS. WATER RESISTANCE.

Underwater Vision

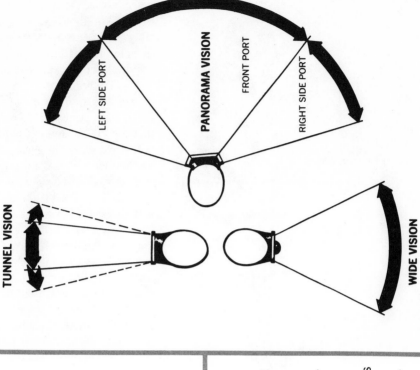

PANORAMA VISION

LEFT SIDE PORT

FRONT PORT

RIGHT SIDE PORT

TUNNEL VISION

WIDE VISION

FITTING THE MASK

- PLACE MASK ON FACE WITH GENTLE SUPPORT.
- INHALE.
- IF MASK REMAINS WITH LITTLE INHALE EFFORT, THE MASK FITS.
- IF THE MASK FALLS OFF OR AIR LEAKS ABOUT THE EDGES, THE MASK DOES NOT FIT.

MASK CHARACTERISTICS

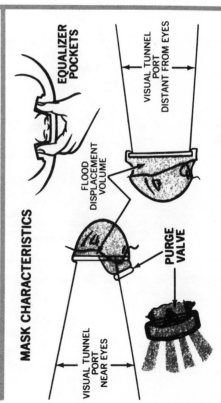

EQUALIZER POCKETS

VISUAL TUNNEL PORT DISTANT FROM EYES

FLOOD DISPLACEMENT VOLUME

PURGE VALVE

VISUAL TUNNEL PORT NEAR EYES

▲ Air tank and demand regulator are the basic pieces of equipment you need to convert a snorkeling outfit into diving gear.

▲ Fins turn your feet into an efficient means of propulsion under water.

ually visible to the snorkeler or "skin" diver. Skin diving with mask, fins, and possibly a wet suit and fish spear, can be just as much fun as scuba diving and it doesn't require a lot of expensive equipment.

While there's no formal certification course for snorkeling, most people learn the fundamentals of this skill before they take up scuba diving. Actually, it's essential, because the important basics of scuba are first learned while using only fins, mask and snorkel. And snorkeling in itself can be great fun. Even if the diver never graduates to the world of scuba, he can still have terrific fun snorkeling along the surface, taking a deep breath, then diving for a submerged object or for a closer look at a fish. The average snorkeler can, on one breath, descend to a depth of 15 to 20 feet and stay there from 20 to 60 seconds. But the greatest excitement, challenge and stimulation in diving lies in the prolonged "downtime" and mobility possible only through taking a certification course and developing a life-long proficiency in diving with scuba equipment.

Rule one of scuba is: never dive alone. During and after training, you should always have a "buddy" for maximum enjoyment both in sharing underwater beauty and experiences, and for safety.

Contrary to popular belief, it's not necessary to dive tremendous depths to enjoy scuba. The first 30 feet of water are the most beautiful because here is where vegetation abounds in the most brilliant colors due to the bright sunlight at this depth. As you go deeper, water filters out light, and colors eventually fade into grays as though you were in a black and white world.

In a day's time, an average scuba diver making water entry from a boat which is outfitted with an air compressor can use from two to three tanks of air for a total of two to three hours of underwater beauty which is never repeated from dive to dive. And even if a boat is unavailable, one usu-

breathing through a tube while the face is underwater. By using a snorkel, it's possible to swim long distances without once lifting one's head. This means the underwater terrain and marine life can remain contin-

How to Get Started Snorkeling or Scuba Diving

◄ Snorkeling is far less expensive than scuba diving and can be just as much fun. When it's cold, you can wear a suit and if you want to fish you can use a spear gun, just as with scuba.

▼ Never snorkel or scuba dive alone. Companions can check each other's gear, keep watch on each other and help in emergencies.

▲ Underwater photography is a rewarding hobby. There are cameras designed for the purpose and a wide variety of equipment to adapt most cameras for use beneath the waves.

ally can enter the water from the beach. In these cases, air for successive beach dives may be available at a nearby dive shop, or you can simply bring along an extra set of filled tanks, or even use double-tank rigs.

Once underwater, many activities present themselves, including shallow wreck diving, photography, hunting artifacts, collecting shells, studying marine life from a vantage point of several feet, spearfishing and the taking of lobsters.

Almost every person in this country already is, or can become physically qualified to do scuba diving. A popular misconception about scuba is that the sport requires superhuman stamina, bulging muscles and abounds with extreme danger at every turn. The truth is, over 90 percent of the swimming population would be able to pass a water proficiency test required for a scuba certification course. Scuba, however, is quite dangerous if a person tries it without proper training, but once proper instruction is obtained, it's much safer than driving a car or even walking across the street.

Many clubs and diving organizations offer scuba travel "packages" to families and individuals. Many divers today take their recreational vehicles and diving equipment on extended trips to Mexico and rely totally on the sea for their food during the stay. Now, more than 25 travel agencies book nothing but tours throughout the world and to the most exotic islands in Pacific/Caribbean waters. The tours are offered at group rates, thus are surprisingly economical, especially for families. And camping is a "natural" for those who choose to avoid commercial areas.

On the community level, some diving clubs own converted school or Greyhound buses for their diving excursions. They'll meet and drive 300 to 500 miles one-way on a weekend diving trip. Again, camping is their most economical means of lodging.

For persons wishing to stay at attractive hotels throughout the world, there are dozens of them catering especially to divers. These facilities furnish diving guides, boats, and top-notch scuba gear including tanks, regulators and weight belts. Generally, guests prefer bringing along their favorite fins, mask and snorkel, though this gear, too, is available if desired.

In California and Nevada many campers are traveling the high Sierras and mountains in search of gold and silver nuggets lying on the bottom of old mining streams. For this activity, the scuba diver has an advantage over land-locked prospectors because he can reach into underwater crevices and actually see between submerged rocks to locate pieces of precious metal lying there.

In some cases, these combination scuba divers and campers become so engrossed and successful in scuba mining, they'll purchase underwater dredges and actually scour miles of river bottom in the mother-lode country.

Naturally, such mobility in remote areas requires that they camp on the river bed, near the site being mined, and in doing this, much use is made of old, forgotten wilderness trails once heavily traveled by prospectors and mules pulling out loads of gold ore.

For camping enthusiasts everywhere in the country, there's either a lake or water-filled quarry within reasonable driving distance. This non-ocean diving, such as in the south and midwest, is popular because the water is spring-fed and clear, thus ideal for photography and observation of game fish. In addition, one can explore wrecks of small boats, discarded autos, antique machinery and rock quarry heavy equipment, or simply pass silently above vast submerged grass fields which abound with marine life in waters less than 15 feet deep. In short, no matter where you base your camp, you're pretty certain to find a good place to scuba dive nearby.

See also: SAFETY, WATER; SWIMMING.

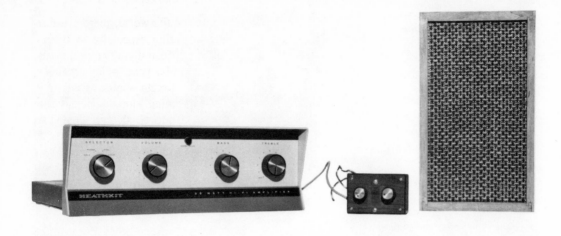

Attention-getting Alarm Generator

**Few can ignore the loud
yelping sound of this electronic
alarm generator.
You can hook it up to your
home security system, or just
experiment with the
variety of sounds it can make**

WHATEVER YOUR INTEREST, burglar alarm to wake-up alarm, here's an electronic alarm generator with an extra low-frequency modulation oscillator that produces a "yelp-yelp-yelp" that's sure to attract plenty of attention.

Both the pitch and repetition rate of this generator are variable over a wide range, so you can create other unusual sounds. If you want to experiment with the circuit, you will probably discover other hookups that give stranger sounds.

This electronic alarm generator is easy to build. The parts are all common and inexpensive. There are no uncommon integrated circuits to buy, and you will probably have most of the parts in your junkbox.

If not, you shouldn't have to spend more than a few dollars for new parts. The construction is very easy. The parts layout is noncritical and you can build it in any way, shape, or form you wish. This generator uses two unijunction transistor oscillators which are DC coupled to produce the strange sounds.

Electronically, the first oscillator (which consists of C1, Q1, R1, R2 and R3) generates a series of low frequency pulses. The output of this oscillator appears across R3 as a corresponding series of voltage fluctuations. R3 also biases the second oscillator (consisting of C3, C4, Q2, R4, R5 and R6) to a point just below oscillation. This resistor must be adjusted to suit the charac-

2328

> Locate parts on this photo-
graph as you assemble them.

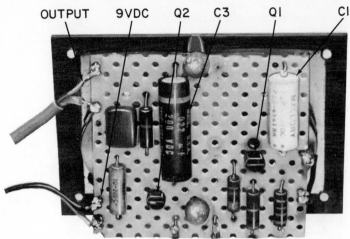

Great for attention-getting
emergency type alarms.

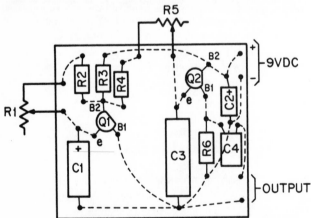

Top view of the electronic alarm generator.
Dashed lines represent wiring underneath a
completed board. Unit will drive headphones.

teristics of the unijunction used for Q2. As
the voltage across R3 drops, it will reach a
level where the second oscillator fires and
its output frequency starts to rise with the
voltage. As the voltage across R3 increases,
the output frequency stops. Potentiometer
R1 controls the repetition rate of the output, while pot R5 controls the frequency.

Putting it together. This version was built
from a 1⅞ x 2¼-inch scrap of perfboard and enclosed in a mini-case. This
arrangement worked very well and you
might want to duplicate it.

Start construction by laying out the ca-
pacitors on the perfboard. Note that C1 and
C4 are positioned near the ends of the
board. Next, insert all of the resistors but
R3. The value of R3 will probably have to
be optimized by experiment, so just ignore
it for now. In this version, potentiometers
R1 and R5 were left off the board to save
space. These pots are mounted on the front
panel of the box and connected to the circuit via short leads. You should now be
able to wire up most of the circuit, and you
might want to add push-in terminals for
the pots, output, and power leads. These
terminals will make external connections to
the board much easier.

When you have finished the wiring, insert the unijunctions. Be careful to check

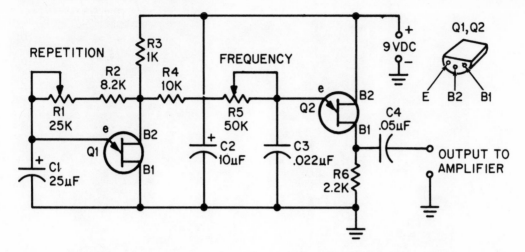

out the leads on your particular unijunctions before you solder them in. The location of the E, B1, and B2 leads may vary with the type of unijunction you use.

Finish the construction by "working" the box. Drill two ¼-inch holes in one side of the box for the power and output leads. Next, the front panel: drill two holes for the pots and two holes to mount the board. Clean up the panel and apply decals if you wish. Install the two pots and temporarily wire them to the rest of the circuit with long leads. Also connect the power and output leads to the module. This completes your mechanical construction of the generator.

Putting it to work. In place of R3 connect a series combination of 330-ohm resistor and a 5000-ohm pot. Connect a pair of 2000-ohm headphones or the AUX input of an amplifier-speaker combination) to the output and connect a 9-volt power supply to the power leads. Now adjust the pot until you get a good sound. If all's well, you should be able to get an attention grabbing sound by adjusting the pots on the front panel. If not, try interchanging the unijunctions. When you are satisfied with the results, remove the pot/resistor combination, measure it with an ohmmeter, and replace it with a resistor of the closest value.

In operation, this electronic alarm generator works very well as an alarm device with just headphones as a reproducer. If your application calls for more volume, connect it to an amplifier.   G.M.C.

See also: ALARMS, BURGLAR; ELECTRONICS; HOME SECURITY SENSORS.

PARTS LIST	
C1	25 µF electrolytic capacitor, 12 VDC or better (Allied Radio 926-1547 or equivalent)
C2	10 µF electrolytic capacitor, 12 VDC or better (Radio Shack 272-1002 or equivalent)
C3	0.022 µF tabular capacitor, 50 VDC or better (Radio Shack 272-1056 or equivalent)
C4	0.05 µF capacitor, 12 VDC or better (Radio Shack 272-1068 or equivalent)
Q1, Q2	Unijunction transistors, exact type not critical (Radio Shack 276-111)
R1	25,000-ohm potentiometer, linear taper (Radio Shack 271-094 or equivalent)
R2	8,200-ohm, ½-watt resistor (Radio Shack 271-000 or equivalent)
R3	1000-ohm, ½-watt resistor, see text (Radio Shack 271-000 or equivalent)
R4	10,000-ohm, ½-watt resistor (Radio Shack 271-000 or equivalent)
R5	50,000-ohm potentiometer, linear taper (Radio Shack 271-1716 or equivalent)
R6	2,200-ohm, ½-watt resistor (Radio Shack 271-000 or equivalent)
Misc.	Perfboard, knobs, spacers, wire, solder, case (Radio Shack 270-230), 9-volt battery or power supply, etc.

Movable Drop Leaf Server

This handsome server has capacious room for linen and silver and opens out to provide a 78-inch length of serving space. You can build it in a weekend

THIS ELEGANT SERVER measures 48 inches long but stretches to 78 inches when the leaves are extended. There is ample room for any occasion, whether it be a banquet or family gathering.

The three roomy drawers can be used for storage of linens and silver. The two compartments will hold plenty of tableware and appliances and, if necessary, they can be fitted with shelves. The original was made without shelves. Sturdy lid supports fold flat when not in use and the hidden casters are handy allowing the large piece to be moved about with ease.

Construction is basic with butt joints

used throughout. The raised panel is easily accomplished on the table saw and the shaped edges are done with a router.

The lumber used is common Idaho pine which is available in most lumberyards in glued up stock to 24 inches wide. This server requires 18-inch material. Choose flat boards and avoid boards with loose knots. The knots are not objectionable, but they should be sound and free of sap.

Since the new lumber sizes have been in effect, you will find that 18-inch stock measures actually 17¼-inch so don't be confused when looking over the materials list. Likewise, one inch stock measures ¾-inch. Therefore, 1-inch x 18-inch really measures ¾-inch x 17¼ inch.

In looking over the drawings, you will note that the top is doubled. This makes for a sturdier piece and it also facilitates assembly. Cleats are eliminated and you won't have to drive nails or screws through the top surface.

Cut the boards to size as per the specifi-

Movable Drop Leaf Server   *2331*

cations. If you purchased long boards, it would be best to rough cut them to size with a portable saw or you may want to use a saber saw to part the large sections. It's a little slower, but much safer. If a board sags toward the end of the cut when using a portable, the tool could kick and this could be dangerous. The saber saw will not kick. This doesn't mean that the portable saw should not be used, but use it only when necessary. As a matter of fact, the saw is ideally suited to trim the boards after they have been rough cut, if you do not have a

radial arm saw. If you use the portable saw, clamp a guide strip on your work to assure a smooth straight cut.

If you use the radial arm saw, chances are that it will not cut the full width of your boards, but with a little ingenuity you can do it. Set the fence to the rear-most position then make the cut. Draw the arm forward as far as it will travel, then if the cut is not completed, carefully raise the leading edge of the panel up slowly until the board separates. Keep fingers clear of the blade.

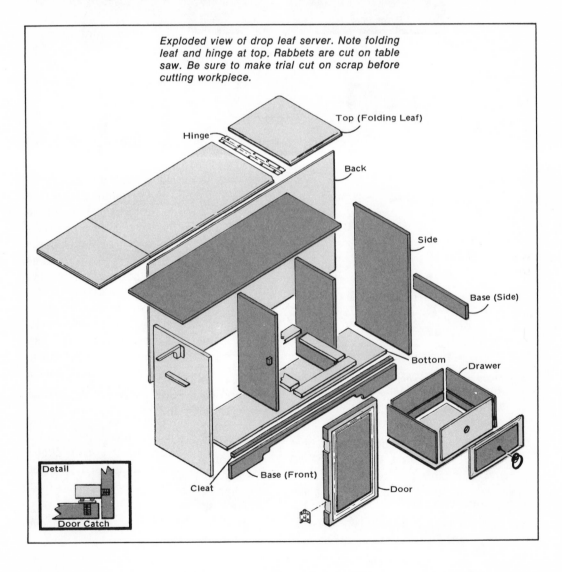

Exploded view of drop leaf server. Note folding leaf and hinge at top. Rabbets are cut on table saw. Be sure to make trial cut on scrap before cutting workpiece.

Top (Folding Leaf)

Hinge

Back

Side

Base (Side)

Bottom

Drawer

Detail

Door Catch

Cleat

Base (Front)

Door

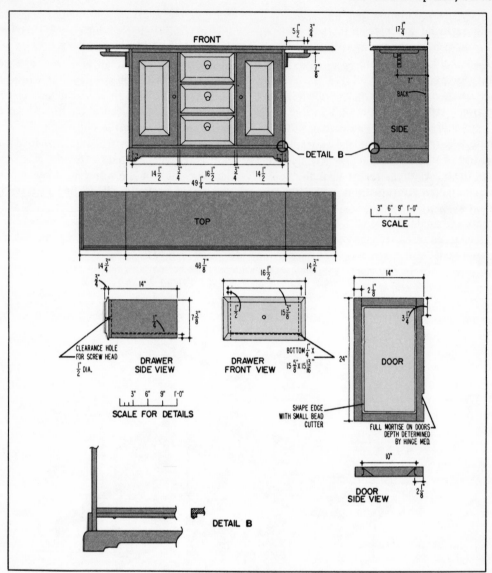

▲ *Clamps are handy when gluing drawer module. Drop leaf hardware is mounted with screws. The units come in pairs—left and right.*

After the boards are cut to size, rabbet the rear edges to take the ¼-inch plywood panel. Use a table saw or router. If the table saw is used, set the height of the blade ¼-inch above the table and the fence ⅜-inch away from the blade. Make the first pass holding the work vertically. The sec-ond pass with the blade readjusted and the work held horizontally will remove the stock forming the rabbet. Assemble the parts with glue and nails. The nails will be concealed by the drop leaf at the top and the apron at the bottom. Before assembly, it would be wise to cut the rear panel, which can then be used to keep the cabinet case square while the glue sets. Simply insert it temporarily with a few brads then remove after the glue has set.

The drawer compartments are built up as a separate modular unit, then inserted into the previously assembled case. Be sure to keep the unit square during assembly. Bar clamps are useful to hold the parts but not essential. If you use nails to hold the sections, try cement-coated finishing nails. They hold very well and will not work loose. The best combination, however, is the use of screws and glue, especially if you lack the bar clamps.

Install the drawer compartment centering it within the main case. Use glue on all joints and again, fasten with nails or screws.

The apron at the base of the cabinet is now added. Use a saber saw or jig saw to cut the scallop in the front piece. When the two side pieces and front have been cut and before installation, run a router fitted with a rounding cutter over the edges to break the sharp corners. Assemble the side pieces by driving screws from the inside of the side panels. The front apron is fastened by means of a cleat, as shown.

The top board and drop leaves should be cut from the same board, if possible. This will assure continuity in the grain pattern and is especially important if the unit is to be stained. Cut the parts, then shape the edge with a suitable router cutter, followed by a good sanding especially at the square edges where the leaves and top met.

To apply the piano hinges, place the top and leaf sections upside down on a clean flat surface. Pull sections together and mark the location of the screw holes. Install a few screws and check the fit. If okay, add the rest of the screws. Now add the wood spacer to the underside of each leaf, then fasten the top to cabinet. The drop leaf hinges are now installed. With leaf in open position and the leaf up, locate the mounting holes for the hinge. Drill pilot holes, then install the hinge. Repeat for other side. Note that the drop leaf hinges come in a set—one left and one right one.

The doors are simple in construction. Cut the frame pieces and assemble with dowels and glue. Use one dowel per corner and be sure to keep the surfaces flat when gluing. When the glue has set, rabbet the backside of the frame to take the raised panel. Perhaps it would be best to wait until the panels are cut before proceeding with this step.

The door panels are cut to size then the saw blade is tilted 15° and raised 1¼-inch. Set the fence so that the saw leaves a $\frac{1}{16}$-inch step on the surface of the board (see drawing). To assure proper fit, cut a trial piece on scrap wood before cutting the doors. When the panels have been cut, rabbet the door frame so that the back of the panel is flush with the door frame.

▲ *If your work is too wide for your saw, raise the wood at the end of the cut, or reverse the piece to complete the cut.*

▲ *As shown here, a gauge block is clamped at the bottom of the side member which assures alignment during assembly.*

⬆ *The drawer divider is assembled as a separate unit. You should check for squareness after assembly is completed.*

⬆ *The panel raising is done by setting the blade at 15° and then feeding as shown. Be sure to feed the work slowly.*

⬆ *Here door frames are rabbeted after assembly. The rabbet is made deep enough to hold the raised panel.*

⬆ *The panels are fitted to the door frames from the rear. The corners of the panels are then rounded to match the rabbet.*

Movable Drop Leaf Server

▲ *Doors are hung with clearance at the top and bottom. Hinge is mortised only in door and flush mounted on the frame.*

▲ *Pictured here is the drop leaf support which is mounted with sufficient space to clear the strip hinge.*

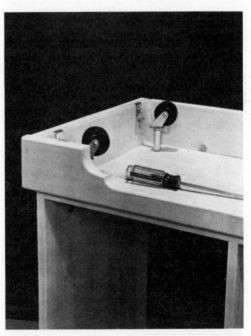

▲ *Drawer bottoms of 1/4-inch plywood slide into dadoes cut into side panels. Sides are cut from medium density overlay.*

▲ *View of self-aligning casters which make the unit mobile and easy to use. Mount them with round head screws.*

MATERIALS LIST		
Quantity	**Size and Description**	**Purpose**
2	$^3/_4''$ $16^1/_4''$x$29^1/_4''$ pine	sides
2	$^3/_4''$ $16^1/_4''$x46$''$ pine	bottom and sub-top
1	$^3/_4''$ $17^1/_4''$x$48^7/_8''$ pine	top
2	$^3/_4''$ $14^3/_4''$x$17^1/_4''$ pine	top ends
2	$^3/_4''$ 16$''$x$24^1/_8''$ pine	uprights
4	$^3/_4''$ $2^5/_{16}''$x$16^1/_2''$ pine	front and rear shelf supports
4	$^3/_4''$ $1^3/_8''$x$11^3/_8''$ pine	side shelf supports
2	$^3/_4''$ $3^3/_4''$x$16^1/_4''$ pine	apron side
1	$^3/_4''$ $3^3/_4''$x$48^3/_4''$ pine	apron front
1	$^3/_4''$ 1$''$x42$''$ pine	apron cleat
1	$^1/_4''$ $24^3/_4''$x$46^5/_8''$ plywood	rear panel
2	$^3/_4''$ $^7/_8''$x$11^5/_8''$ pine	drop leaf spacer
3	$^3/_4''$ $7^5/_{16}''$x$16^7/_{16}''$ pine	drawer front
6	$^1/_2''$ $7^3/_8''$x$15^3/_8''$ plywood	drawer sub-front and rear
6	$^1/_2''$ $7^3/_8''$x14$''$ plywood	drawer sides
4	$^3/_4''$ $2^1/_8''$x24$''$ pine	door frame sides
4	$^3/_4''$ $2^1/_8''$x$9^3/_4''$ pine	door frame top and bottom
2	$^3/_4''$ 10$''$x20$''$ pine	door panel
2	1$''$x$16^1/_4''$ continuous hinge	
4	$1^3/_8''$x2$''$ door hinge	

NOTE: Also need casters, catches, pulls, knobs, drop leaf brackets and finishing materials.

The rabbeting of the frame will leave a radius at each corner. This can be left as is and the raised panels rounded to match, or the rounded corners can be cut square with a chisel. Apply a bead of glue in the rabbet, then insert the panel and clamp.

Mortise the doors to accept the full depth of the hinges. The hinges are then flush mounted on the side panels.

The drawers are made as per drawing. The front panels are raised as were the door pieces. Before adding the front piece to the drawers, drill ½-inch clearance holes to allow clearance for the drawer hardware. Fasten the fronts with 1-inch round head screws and glue. Place stops at the rear of the drawer compartments to limit the travel of the drawers.

Sand the entire cabinet then add the casters and door catch hardware. Finish as desired. The server shown here was finished with two coats of latex antique base paint.   J.C.

See also: CABINETS; CHINA CABINET; EARLY AMER- ICAN; FINISHING, WOOD; FURNITURE, INDOOR; PARSONS TABLE; TABLES; WOODWORKING.

WHERE TO FIND IT

If your local supplier does not have them, drop leaf brackets are available from the Armor Company, Box 290, Deer Park, N. Y. 11729. Write to them for information.

Build a Roll-about Server

This handy buffet server rolls about on casters and is fun to make

THIS HANDSOME BUFFET SERVER is mounted on casters and can be easily rolled to where the action is. This is especially appreciated when you have a large gathering on holidays and special occasions. The double top and roomy compartment below make this a very versatile and important piece of furniture.

The corner posts can be made first. Choose a close-grained hardwood such as poplar. The stock should be fairly flat and free of defects. Unless you can obtain 2¼-inch square stock, you will have to glue up two pieces of 1⅛-inch stock. This is commonly referred to as 5/4 (five quarters). Most lumberyards carry this, but if they don't you can have them order it for you.

Cut the pieces slightly oversize, then glue them up using a suitable glue. White glue is fine and easy to use. Coat both surfaces, then slide the pieces together, and clamp until the glue sets. To prevent shifting, drive a nail at each end in the waste area. This will keep the pieces from sliding while

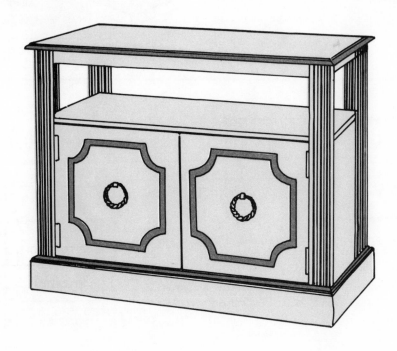

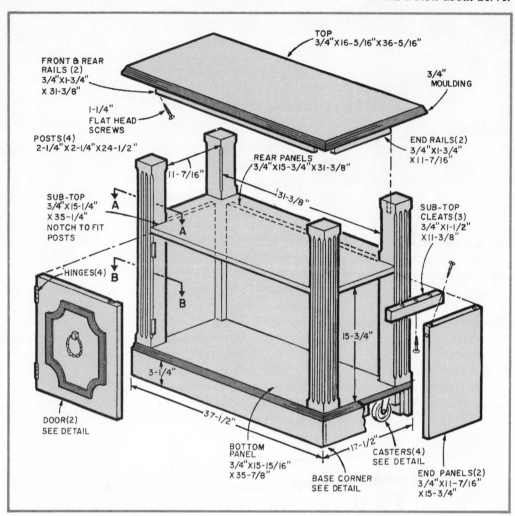

TOP
3/4"X16-5/16"X36-5/16"

FRONT & REAR
RAILS (2)
3/4"X1-3/4"
X 31-3/8"

3/4"
MOULDING

1-1/4"
FLAT HEAD
SCREWS

POSTS(4)
2-1/4"X 2-1/4"X24-1/2"

END RAILS(2)
3/4"X1-3/4"
X11-7/16"

11-7/16"

REAR PANELS
3/4"X15-3/4"X31-3/8"

SUB-TOP
3/4"X15-1/4"
X 35-1/4"
NOTCH TO FIT
POSTS

31-3/8"

SUB-TOP
CLEATS (3)
3/4"X1-1/2"
X11-3/8"

HINGES(4)

15-3/4"

3-1/4"

DOOR(2)
SEE DETAIL

37-1/2"

BOTTOM
PANEL
3/4"X15-15/16"
X 35-7/8"

17-1/2"

CASTERS(4)
SEE DETAIL

BASE CORNER
SEE DETAIL

END PANELS(2)
3/4"X11-7/16"
X 15-3/4"

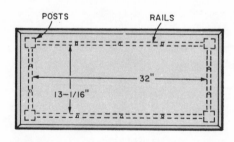

POSTS   RAILS

32"

13-1/16"

▲ *Top held on rails (dotted lines) by screws.*

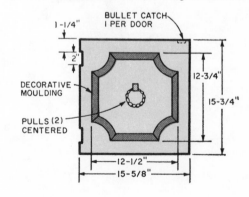

▼ *Decorative handles and molding trim doors.*

BULLET CATCH
1 PER DOOR

1-1/4"

2"

12-3/4"

15-3/4"

DECORATIVE
MOULDING

PULLS (2)
CENTERED

12-1/2"

15-5/8"

Build a Roll-about Server 2339

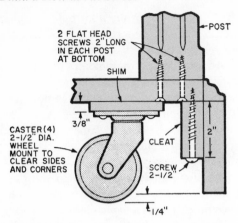

2 FLAT HEAD
SCREWS 2" LONG
IN EACH POST
AT BOTTOM

POST

SHIM

CASTER (4)
2-1/2" DIA.
WHEEL
MOUNT TO
CLEAR SIDES
AND CORNERS

3/8"

CLEAT

2"

SCREW
2-1/2"

1/4"

⚑ *Shim thickness adjusted to place casters, concealed in base, to clear carpet pile.*

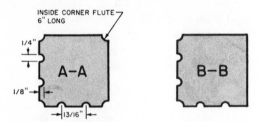

INSIDE CORNER FLUTE
6" LONG

1/4"

A-A

1/8"

13/16"

B-B

⚑ *Corner post fluting as shown on 2 sides.*

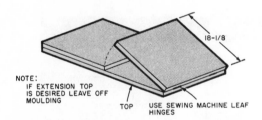

NOTE:
IF EXTENSION TOP
IS DESIRED LEAVE OFF
MOULDING

18-1/8

TOP

USE SEWING MACHINE LEAF
HINGES

⚑ *Delete molding on ends, if you add optional extension leaves to table top.*

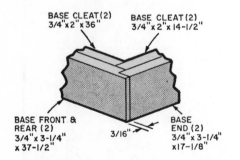

BASE CLEAT (2)
3/4"x 2"x 36"

BASE CLEAT (2)
3/4"x 2"x 14-1/2"

BASE FRONT &
REAR (2)
3/4"x 3-1/4"
x 37-1/2"

3/16"

BASE
END (2)
3/4"x 3-1/4"
x17-1/8"

⚑*Rabbeted ends and molding help to finish base and make a professional looking job.*

clamping pressure is applied. When the glue has set, trim the posts to length. Next, plane the sides of the block to true them up. This is best done on a planer or joiner. If you lack these machines, you can use a block or jack plane.

Fluting the posts is done with a router fitted with a round-nose bit. With a pencil and square, draw light guide lines one inch from the ends. Clamp a guide block on the router base then cut the flutes. Stop the cuts when the bit reaches the pencil lines. Note that the flutes are cut on two faces only. Also note that the inside corner does not run the length of the post. It is only six inches long.

The wood used for the cabinet is lumber core. Several choices are available according to your own taste. The server shown here was made from red birth which has a pleasing grain pattern and is close grained. Normally the back of a cabinet of this sort is closed off with a less expensive grade of wood and left unfinished. Not so in this case. Because the buffet is mounted on casters and is portable, the rear side must be made with cabinet wood and finished accordingly.

Cut the pieces to size on the table saw. If you have a plywood blade, use it for it will produce a nice clean cut which will require no further treatment. The sub-top is notched to fit between the corner posts. Notches are best cut on the table saw.

After the bottom panel has been cut, mount the corner posts using glue and screws. Two screws in each corner will suffice. Next mount the end and rear panels. These are held with screws through the bottom and top.

The top screws are mounted diagonally into the posts. Rather than sinking the screw heads, blind clearance holes are drilled on the underside of the sub-top. This will make for a stronger joint.

With end and rear panels in place, the base section can be made up. Rip the 3¼-

inch width, then carefully cut the lengths to size. The ends are rabbeted as indicated and the pieces are joined with white glue. The cleats that line the base are pre-drilled for the screw clearance holes, then they are assembled with nails and glue. Use 1½-inch nails and drive them at a slight angle so they won't protrude from the face.

Attach the base to the main section with screws, then apply the nose and cove molding. Use 1-inch brads and glue. Sink the brads and fill with wood putty. The sub-top is installed using cleats. The top is made up by adding the rails before assembly. Check the location and position of the rails to make sure there is proper clearance at the corners for the posts. Diagonal screws through the rail corners into the posts hold the top firmly. Use glue. Add the molding to the outer edge of the top and check the miters carefully before assembly.

The doors are cut with matching grain. Mortise out the area for the hinges according to the drawing. Note that the gain for the hinges is cut in the door only. In other words, the gain is mortised only in the door for the full thickness of the butt hinge.

Add the decorative moldings to the doors with glue. Brads are not necessary. Be careful not to use too much glue. Do not allow it to ooze out from the edges. Apply the glue only to the center of the molding and spread with a glue brush or with your finger. If necessary, wipe away any excess. Light pencil guide lines will help you position the pieces. If any glue squeezes out, wipe quickly with a damp cloth.

The swivel casters are mounted so the base rests 3 inches above the floor (more if the server is to be used in a room with a rug). Use spacer blocks to allow the wheels to protrude a sufficient amount.

Stain and finish the cabinet as desired. Add the hardware and bring on the food.   J.C.

See also: CABINETS; CHINA CABINET; EARLY AMERICAN; FINISHING, WOOD; FURNITURE, INDOOR; WOODWORKING.

MATERIALS LIST

Quantity	Size and Description	Purpose
1	³/₄″ 16⁵/₁₆″x36⁵/₁₆″ birch	top
2	³/₄″ 1³/₄″x11⁷/₁₆″ birch	end rails
2	³/₄″ 1³/₄″x31³/₈″ birch	front and rear rails
4	2¹/₄″ 2¹/₄″x24¹/₂″ poplar	posts
1	³/₄″ 15¹/₄″x35¹/₄″ birch	sub-top
1	³/₄″ 15¹⁵/₁₆″x35⁷/₈″ birch	bottom
2	³/₄″ 11⁷/₁₆″x15³/₄″ birch	ends
2	³/₄″ 15⁵/₈″x15³/₄″ birch	doors
1	³/₄″ 15³/₄″x31³/₈″ birch	rear panel
2	³/₄″ 3¹/₄″x17¹/₈″ birch	base ends
2	³/₄″ 3¹/₄″x37¹/₂″ birch	base front and rear
3	³/₄″ 1¹/₂″x11³/₈″ pine	sub-top cleats
2	³/₄″ 2″x14¹/₂″ pine	base cleats
2	³/₄″ 2″x36″ pine	base cleats

NOTE: Also need nose and cove molding, decorative molding, door pulls, butt hinges, bullet catches, swivel casters, screws, glue, brads, nails and finishing material.

Sharp Edges Make Short Work

How to give your knives and axes a professional edge

FEW CASUAL CAMPERS seem to have learned the art of tool sharpening. Yet, for most tools, the procedure is a simple, easy and actually pleasant experience. Good woodsmen take pride in the edges they have put on their knives, axes, saws and digging tools. They know that the sharper the edge the easier their work.

This doesn't mean that a sportsman's tools must have razor sharp edges. In fact, on most tools, a hair-splitting edge is actually undesirable. Sharpness is a relative thing and there is an edge to suit the purpose a tool is used for. For example: two woodcarvers, using identical knives, but working with woods of different hardness, may each prefer entirely different degrees of sharpness. They obtain their personal preference in edges by doing the job themselves.

No edge is smooth. Some are just less rough than others. Any good cutting edge looks like a tiny saw, because all blades are used with something akin to a sawing ac-

tion. Without those peaks and valleys your blade is dull.

The best grades of properly tempered tool steel have a high degree of flexibility which extends into the sawlike teeth. Being flexible, the teeth bend back and forth under use and gradually break away. When they are completely gone, the blade is dull and ready for oilstoning. Never stone a cutting edge without using some kind of lubricant on the stone.

Any light weight oil will do. If oil is not available, use water. The stone must be lubricated. This lets the ground-off particles of steel from your blade float away without "gumming" the stone. The oil also keeps things cool. Considerable heat is generated, even in hand stoning, and it is easier than you think to actually "burn" a fine blade, destroying its temper.

Oilstones come in many shapes and sizes. Some are long and lean, some round and short, some curved; even concave and convex ones to suit whatever sharpening job

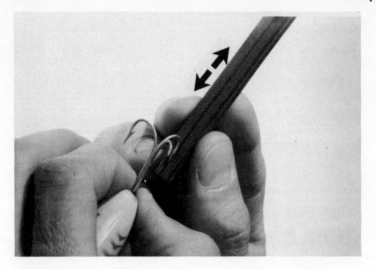

◄ Sharpening fish hooks. Specially designed stone has three grooved sides and a flat side. Sharpening of tips and barbs is done by drawing them back and forth in grooves. Sharpen sides by rotating sides of barbs over flat side of stone while moving stone lengthwise, both up and down.

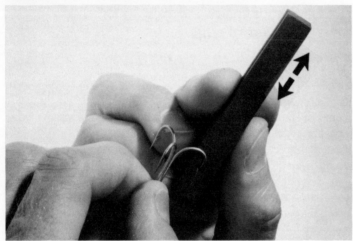

◄ Use stone with coarse and fine sides to sharpen your hunting knife. Spread oil on coarse side, place the blade flat on stone in slight diagonal. Tip back up about 30°. Draw blade against stone diagonally from heel to tip several strokes. Flop blade, stone, repeat the above process.

◄ *Axes need strong, obtuse wedge-shaped edge. Lubricate stone, hold axe on horizontal support with cutting edge projecting. Stroke the axe blade with circular motions at about 45° from axis of head. First use the coarse side of the stone, then flip stone and use the fine edge to sharpen.*

▼ *For pocket knives, spread oil on stone, hold stone by one end at corner of flat surface. Place blade flat on stone in diagonal position. Tip up back of blade about 30°. Draw blade against stone diagonally beginning at heel and ending at tip of the stone for best results.*

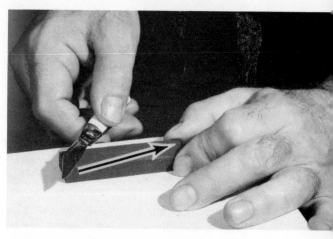

is at hand. Oilstones also come in various degrees of hardness and grit sizes. There are soft, medium and hard stones; coarse, medium and fine stones. There are also natural stones.

Basically, there are three types of edges to which various tools are stoned.

Coarse-edged tools include the majority of implements used by the outdoorsman: some knives, scythes, sickles, brush hooks, axes, spades, shovels, etc.

Medium-edged tools include those used by mechanics: knives, chisels, plane irons, drawknives, stockmaker's and woodcarver's gouges and knives. You may prefer a medium edge on a hunting knife for careful skinning, as when skinning a trophy or for thin-skinned birds and animals.

The third type, fine-edge, is reserved almost exclusively for specialized instruments: razors and blades used in surgery, dentistry, biological dissection and other delicate work.

There is, therefore, a definite relationship between the tool and its intended use and the stone, or stones, used for sharpening.

The very keenest edges are obtained with the natural stones, the well-known Novaculite Hard Arkansas being the hardest, finest

and therefore capable of producing the "smoothest" of edges. The Arkansas are finish stones. They are used after preliminary sharpening has been completed on less fine, less hard grits, and for touching up slightly dulled fine-edged blades.

The ultimate in edge smoothness is achieved by "stropping" the blade on a leather strap, or strop.

Good knives are of the hollow ground or semi-hollow ground variety. Any good knife will have this hollow ground taper from back to cutting edge. The "hollow" reduces the amount of unneeded steel, while at the same time, maintaining rigidity of the blade. Semi-hollow ground blades are nearly ideal for general sportsman use. All blades have a bevel, or sharper taper, near the edge. This is the part that requires stoning. But first you must have an oilstone.

A combination stone of coarse and fine silicon carbide is a good choice for general sharpening of knives, cleavers, scissors, plane irons, drawknives, axes and hatchets. It's an all around stone at a moderate price. The coarse side of the stone is used for full sharpening of the coarser tools and is useful for restoring badly dulled edges on the keen-edged ones.

The fine side of the combination stone is used for fine stoning of tools requiring a sharper edge.

If you really want that razor edge on your sheathknife, finish the stoning with a Hard Arkansas stone. A good Hard Arkansas is expensive, but it's worth it if you want a really sharp edge on a fine knife.

If the blade is badly dulled, start with the coarse side of your combination stone. A blade that fails to cut may be brought back to shape on the coarse oilstone.

All stoning is done against the bevel of the blade. That is, with the cutting edge being moved, with light pressure, into the stone as if trying to remove tiny shavings from it. The movement is a diagonal one to utilize the full surface of the stone. This technique keeps the face of the stone flat as it wears, prolonging the stone's useful life.

Spread cutting oil generously over the face of the stone. Place the stone flush with a corner of your bench or table, steadying it with one hand, while holding the tool with the other.

Axes, scythes and sickles, are best sharpened with a rather circular motion of the stone on the tool. The blade is held stationary and the stone is moved over it. This is also the better way of sharpening plated and stainless cutlery to avoid marring the shiny finish of the blade.

Be sure and maintain the factory ground bevel by tilting the blade at such an angle that this bevel is parallel to the stone. Remember, you want only to sharpen the edge of the tool, not reshape the blade.

Keep plenty of oil on the stone during the sharpening and, after every few strokes, test the blade for sharpness. This is best done by very lightly running the ball of one of your fingers along the edge. Use no pressure. If the blade is sharp, you will feel a slight drag. More likely, you will feel alternately smooth and draggy spots. These indicate that, although the sharpening is proceeding, there are uneven spots along the edge. Keep at it. You're getting there.

When the edge begins to feel uniformly sharp from the coarse stoning, switch to the

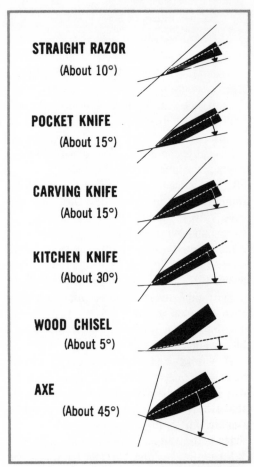

STRAIGHT RAZOR
(About 10°)

POCKET KNIFE
(About 15°)

CARVING KNIFE
(About 15°)

KITCHEN KNIFE
(About 30°)

WOOD CHISEL
(About 5°)

AXE
(About 45°)

⫪ *Drawings highlight wide range of sharpening angles from razor to axe and do not represent tools of any particular manufacturer. These angles give proper support to the metal to prevent frequent dulling or breakdown of cutting edges of various tools.*

SHARPENING TIPS

1. Always wipe off any blade after each use and wipe with oil or other rust inhibitor before storing.

2. If hunting knives are to be stored for some time, it is best to store them unsheathed. Leather covers often pick up salts that cause rusting by moisture absorption.

3. The sharpening stone should be kept clean and moist. To let it dry out or expose it to air tends to harden it.

4. After using stone, the dirty oil should be wiped off and fresh oil applied. The best stones are packed in wood boxes with covers to protect them from the air.

5. Oil prevents glazing of the stone and also acts as a coolant to avoid heat caused by friction.

6. Do not use heavy oils or greases on an oilstone. They fill the pores and cause glazing and gumming. Special stone oils are best, Bear Oil, Buck Oil among them. Kerosene and non-gumming household oils are permissible substitutes.

7. If a stone becomes glazed or gummed up, cleaning it with gasoline or ammonia will often restore its cutting qualities. An excellent cleaner is a 50:50 mixture of ammoniated household cleanser. Soak overnight with stone covered in cleaner. Soak in fresh solution if further soaking is needed. Soak and flush in clean water, then dry in barely warm oven (125°F) for 8 to 10 hours. Soak stone overnight in kerosene or Bear-type oil.

8. Some stones are pre-saturated with oil at the factory. They require only slight further application of oil before each use. Natural stones and many other man-made ones are not so treated. Soak as above before using.

9. Always use the entire surface of the stone. This prevents grooving or uneven wear.

10. The higher priced stones are lifetime investments. With proper care, they will pay for themselves in efficiency to your tools.

fine side of your combination stone. Don't forget the oil.

A blade with a double bevel must be stoned on both sides. Work one side through a stroke or two, then flip the blade over and stone the other. Working both sides evenly.

With a fine oilstone, if the blade is sharpened thoroughly, there will be no perceptible "wire edge," or burr—none at all if the blade is finished on an Arkansas stone.

A wire edge is felt by an upward movement of a finger along the blade edge. A wire edge feels like the blade's edge is somewhat bent to one side. Continued stoning will remove the burr and leave a sharp cutting edge.

Stropping is done by stroking the blade with the grain of the leather strap, rather than against it. Stropping removes the very last of the burr, or wire edge, to give the very keenest of blades.

Only in the case of badly worn or poorly cared for knives will you need to resort to the coarse stone. The fine grit will maintain a high quality, well-sharpened knife for years.

Rarely a bevel will need to be reground. This should not be attempted by the amateur. The heat generated by even well lubricated grinding wheels can destroy the quality of the best of cutlery. If a quality tool ever needs regrinding, take it to a professional or return it to the factory.   J.R.

See also: CHISELS; KNIVES AND AXES; TOOLS.

WHERE TO FIND IT

Suppliers of sharpening equipment include Behr-Manning, Div. of Norton Co., P. O. Box 809, Troy, N. Y. 12181; Buck Knives, Inc., 6588 Federal Blvd., San Diego, Cal. 92114; Gerber Legendary Blades, 14200 S. W. 72nd Ave., Portland, Ore. 97223; Knife Importers, 1325 S. Congress Ave., Austin, Tex. 78767; Randall Made Knives, Box 1988, Orlando, Fla. 32802; and Solingen Cutlery, 4110 La Crescenta Ave., Montrose, Cal. 91020. Write to them for information.

All about Sharpening Stones

**There's a stone for every
sharpening purpose. Here's how
to pick out the right
stone and use it to keep your
cutting edges razor sharp**

ONE CANNOT DENY THE VALUE of a grinding wheel. Every well outfitted shop should have at least one. But abrasive wheels should not be used to do every job. A well planned shop also includes a selection of files and a couple sharpening stones.

For the most part, tools are initially sharpened on a grinding wheel, but most shop or household tools are best resharpened with a whetstone. Even tools which require filing (as does an axe) or burnishing (as does a cabinet scraper) need stone work somewhere along the line. For the small shop, portable stones are less expensive and much safer than grinding wheels and you will be surprised to learn of the variety of jobs best handled with stones.

With two or three stones of different grits or even with one combination grit stone you can quickly sharpen knives, chisels, woodworking tools for lathe or carving, plane blades and axes. The secret is in matching abrasive and technique.

The right abrasive. Not much before the 18th century, experts discovered ways to mix natural abrasive crystals with clay to make harder, better stones. Two crystals, harder than quartz, were used. Emery, basically aluminum oxide in iron oxide

crystals, was the first. Corundum was another. We still use them, but in different ways.

Emery is now used mostly for abrasive papers. It has limited use in wheel grinding but is rarely used for small stones. Corundum is still available, in a better form. Sandstone has limited use. But of the natural abrasives only Arkansas stone, in "hard" and "soft" grits, remains better for fine honing than anything man can devise. For most sharpening jobs man-made abrasives are now best.

The first man-made abrasive came in the early 1890s when silicon carbide was developed by fusing coke and silica sand in electric furnaces. Five years later bauxite was fused electrically to create pure aluminum oxide, a slightly softer material. For many years, silicon carbide was the hardest man-made material available. Not many years ago boron carbide was developed; hardest of all man-made materials, surprisingly close to diamond in toughness.

From the full field of abrasives, three handle most of the work. Aluminum oxide and silicon carbide are most often used in whetstones. Arkansas hard stone is still best for fine edging. Sandstone, most often Ohio

◄ *Bench stone is at left. Center top is slip for rounded tools with knife below it. Right are axe stone, top, Arkansas hard stone.*

▼ *Ideal for straight edges is bench stone. Strop, Arkansas hard stone hone top edges. Small stone, at lower left, is for knives.*

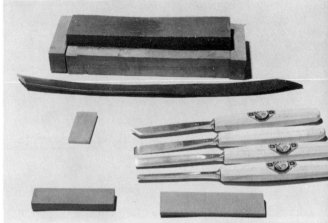

blue stone, is used for low-cost general sharpening stones. All are available in three types—bench stones, files and slips.

Bench stones. Designed for "all-purpose" sharpening, they are excellent for restoring the cutting edge to most straight-edged tools. In aluminum oxide and silicon carbide formulations, can handle nearly any metal. Abrasive files, in square and triangular shapes, are most often used to precision hone exacting equipment, as gears and dies. Slip stones are used to sharpen curved tools and to sharpen special tools such as reamers and augers.

The three types of stones are available in both aluminum oxide and silicon carbide materials in several grits from coarse (or soft) to fine (or hard). You may need only one or two grits in aluminum oxide stones or you may need several grits in two or more materials. Most of the time a couple aluminum oxide stones and an Arkansas stone or two will handle all jobs.

Bench stones are available in single grits and in combination grits, with a medium or coarse grit on one side and a fine on the other. For most shops a combination stone is an excellent bargain.

Many bench stones require oil as a lubricant to make the sharpening easier and as a preservative to protect the stone. Some stones are oil-filled at the factory. Others require soaking before they can be used. If the stone should be oil soaked, the manu-

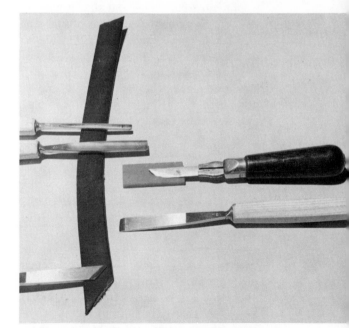

▲ *Fine honing can be done on Arkansas hard stone, center, and on strop (make one from old belt). For a sharp edge, use them both.*

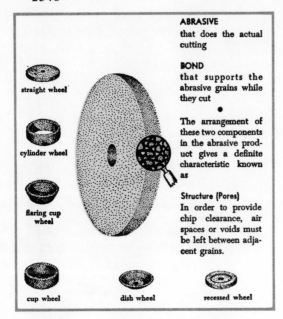

ABRASIVE
that does the actual cutting

BOND
that supports the abrasive grains while they cut

•

The arrangement of these two components in the abrasive product gives a definite characteristic known as

Structure (Pores)
In order to provide chip clearance, air spaces or voids must be left between adjacent grains.

straight wheel

cylinder wheel

flaring cup wheel

cup wheel   dish wheel   recessed wheel

◄ *Every well-equipped shop should have one such grinding wheel. Selected files and a couple of sharpening stones are also needed.*

1. The material and its hardness—use aluminum oxide for steel and steel alloys; silicon carbide for cast iron, non-ferrous metals and non-metallic materials. As with stones, use a fine grit for hard, brittle metals; coarse for soft, ductile materials. Use hard grits for easily penetrated metals; soft grits for hard materials.

2. Be guided by the amount of metal to be removed—use coarse grits for rapid grinding, fine grits for high finish work. Use a grit bonded in vitrified materials for cutting and bonded in "commercial" materials such as rubber, shellac or resinoids for high finish grinding.

3. Be guided by moisture—use a wheel at least one grit harder for wet grinding.

4. Be guided by grinding speeds—vitrified bond abrasives are best for wheels turning less than 6,500 rpm. Use abrasives embedded in rubber, shellac, resinoid (organic bonds) for wheel speeds over 6,500.

5. Be guided by the area of contact—use coarse grits when grinding large areas, use fine grits when grinding small areas.

6. Be guided by the ease of the job—use tough abrasives for hard grinding, use a milder abrasive for light grinding on hard steels.

Care of stones. Grinding wheels are expensive and you can make them last by checking them frequently. The cutting edge should be trued and dressed often. Commercial dressing sticks can clean most wheels, but for precision truing you will need a dressing wheel. The center holes should be inspected, cleaned and oiled often. Whetstones require less care. A few simple hints can help you keep them in top condition.

All abrasive stones are brittle and will

facturer generally includes instructions. Light machine oil or neet's foot oil works best.

Careless workers often interchange aluminum oxide stones and silicon carbide stones, using either for all kinds of sharpening. For the best possible edge be sure to use the right stone. Aluminum oxide stones are best for high quality steel when a keen edge is required. They are ideal for chisels, plane blades and similar tools. Silicon carbide stones are excellent for speed sharpening when a really keen edge is less important. They are most often used by builders for on-the-job sharpening and for sharpening cutlery. When selecting grits follow this basic rule: fine grits are best for hard, brittle metals, coarse grits are better for soft, ductile metals.

Grinding wheels. While these simple rules are all you need to select bench stones, you will want to be more particular when you buy abrasives for your grinder. You can get the right abrasive and the right bond (the material used to keep the abrasive crystals together) if you will follow these six guides:

All about Sharpening Stones

break if you drop them. Protect larger stones with wooden boxes. Oil stones, especially, will last longer if the box has a lid to keep dirt from the surface. The box can be rudimentary, elegant or ready-made. You can make cloth, cardboard or leather pockets for smaller stones.

If the stone is not oil saturated and does require an oil bath before use, give it a brief soaking in light machine oil. Many stones will last longer if you wash them once in a while in warm soap suds. Wipe them dry, then give them a brief soaking in machine oil. Do not oversoak and wipe away excess oil.

A stone should have a flat surface to deliver true, accurate edges. To avoid wearing hollows in any stone, sharpen over the full surface, rather than in the center. Once a stone develops a low center it is nearly always useless for accurate jobs such as plane and chisel blades and may need to be replaced.

How to sharpen. A good edge depends on good sharpening habits. The stone should be fixed to the bench so it will not slide. A box may hold it firm, but if it doesn't, tack strips of wood around the

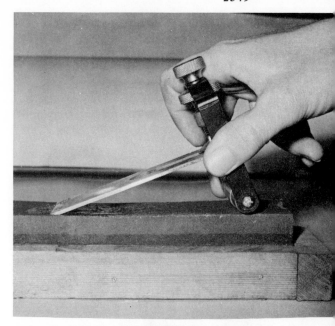

▲ *Mount cutter in plane sharpener for accurate bevel. Blade, so held, adjusted for proper angle with stone, is worked back and forth.*

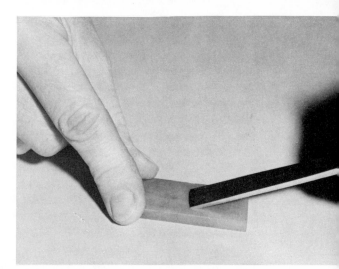

▲ *Hone chisel on Arkansas hard stone for top edge this way. Draw chisel back, forward.*

◄ *Chisel is sharpened on medium grit, finished on fine. Keep bevel edge flat; use oil.*

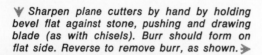 *Sharpen plane cutters by hand by holding bevel flat against stone, pushing and drawing blade (as with chisels). Burr should form on flat side. Reverse to remove burr, as shown.* ▶

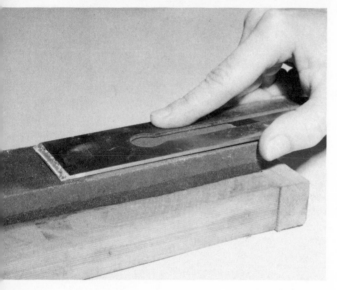

▶ *Sharpen knife as shown in multiple exposure, with circular motion at angle required by the edge bevel. Be sure to use oil on stone.*

All about Sharpening Stones

◄ For keen edge, strop blade on leather after sharpening. Remove all oil first. Emery dust can be worked into your strop to improve it.

▲ Sharpen axe with these tools: round dressing stone (silicon carbide is good) and a file.

stone or the box. Some deluxe shops have stones sunk into the bench top. Keep an oil can with light machine oil or neet's foot oil on hand.

A few tools such as plane cutters and knives may require grinding only when a new bevel is necessary or when the cutting edge is nicked. Grinding can straighten the edge and restore the bevel but the final sharpening should be done on a stone.

When grinding chisels and plane blades (with angles of about 25°), a good rule to remember is that the bevel should be a little longer than twice the thickness of the metal. The grindstone should turn toward the blade. Be sure to check metal temperature often; the chisel or plane blade should not be allowed to overheat. Quench the blade tip often in water to prevent overheating. As you grind, move the blade from side to side to grind all parts of the bevel and to keep the wheel surface true.

When you begin sharpening, assemble all equipment before you work. If the tools are new or very dull, sharpen first on coarse grit stones. Tools which have been used and sharpened before can be sharpened on medium grits or even fine grits. For honing and touch-up use an Arkansas hard stone.

If the whetting is done on an aluminum oxide or Carborundum stone a honing should follow on the Arkansas if a keen edge is important. For a perfect edge remove all oil and strop the blade lightly on leather.   R.L.B.

See also: KNIVES AND AXES; TOOLS.

WRONG

RIGHT

◄ When used for offhand grinding, the mechanical dresser should be supported on a work rest or other rigid support. The gap between the work rest and the wheel should be no wider than necessary. Move the dresser in a straight line across the wheel face, with the heel resting firmly against the edge of the work rest.

How to Keep Tools Sharp

Get into the habit of keeping the cutting edges of your tools in tip-top shape. An occasional honing on a whetstone usually does the trick

THE TOOL THAT HAS LOST its ability to cut, rip, drill or drive is as useless as no tool at all. Do you throw it away and buy a new one? Of course not. Tools are expensive and, besides, before long that new tool would also need a better edge.

For this reason, all home workshop buffs should become familiar with the ways in which professionals sharpen tools and get their working edges back into shape.

There are many tools that need sharpening or renewing of their edges. In dealing with the most common workshop types, the type of tool you have determines how you handle the edge.

For bevel-edged tools such as chisels, plane blades and gouges more often than not, honing of the tool is needed rather than grinding.

To hone chisels and planes, use a honing oilstone. A light oil, such as kerosene or kerosene mixed with light motor oil, is applied to the stone to float particles of steel and keep them from filling the pores of the stone.

Hold the blade with one hand and use other as a guide. Place the beveled edge on the stone with the blade raised to an angle of about 25° to 30°. Move the blade back and forth with a smooth motion.

This action will put a wire or feather edge on the blade. So, turn the blade over and hold its flat side flat on the stone. Take a few strokes, but be sure to avoid holding the blade on an angle, which will bevel the flat side of the blade.

Finish the honing process by stropping the beveled end on a leather strap.

A positive way of telling whether you've made a good edge is to look at the blade. A blade which is dull reflects light; a blade which is sharp doesn't. Hold the blade so light shines on it. If there are no "white" spots reflecting off, you know it is sharp.

The only time it becomes necessary to grind a plane blade or chisel is when the edges and bevel of the tool are badly worn. It is best to do this on a grinding stone driven by an electric motor.

In grinding, hold the bevel of the tool against the stone surface at an angle of 25° to 30°, either by hand or by having the blade clamped in an adjustable grinding device. If by hand, make sure the blade is held absolutely steady to avoid putting a wave in it. Light pressure is used, and the tool is moved from side to side.

If a dry grinding stone is used, dip the tool into cold water frequently so the steel maintains its temper. This is important.

How to Keep Tools Sharp

Again, a wire edge will be formed. A stroke or two of the tool's flat side against an oilstone will get rid of it, followed by stropping on a leather strap.

Cutting Tools such as knives, hatchets, are sharpened against the edge rather than just retaining the bevel, as with chisels. Use either a medium fine oilstone or a sharpening steel, as illustrated. With the oilstone on the bench, move the edge of the blade forward, then turn the blade over and reverse the direction—the edge will still be moving forward on the stone. Use a rotary motion with larger knives to cover the entire length with each stroke. Sharpening with a tempered "steel" is similar, except that the steel is held in the left hand while the blade is stroked outward from the handle, honing one edge at each stroke, then returned to the handle and repeated on the lower side of the steel for the second edge. An alternative is to flip the blade around and complete the stroke from the end back toward the handle. Do each side of the blade an even number of times. Generally, two complete strokes will be sufficient, but develop the habit of stropping the knife frequently, preferably every time it is used—the process takes barely a minute and keeps the knife edge always in keen condition.

Axes and hatchets are sharpened by rotating the stone over both sides of the edge an equal number of times. Lawn mower blades are done the same way. Hatchet heads and power mower blades that are nicked or very dull can be given a new edge by grinding with an abrasive disk tightly chucked into an electric drill. Hold the wheel at the angle that corresponds to the original bevel of the tool, striving for uniform bevel on both sides of the edge.

⋀ Honing a blade removes the fine strip of metal that has curled over the edge. Hold the plane blade so that its beveled edge rests at a 25 to 30 degree angle on the whetstone. Sharpening rig gives better control.

⋀ Grinding is done best when stone has an adjustable tool rest that is set to retain the original bevel.

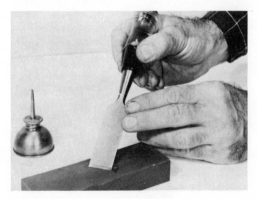

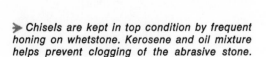

➤ Chisels are kept in top condition by frequent honing on whetstone. Kerosene and oil mixture helps prevent clogging of the abrasive stone.

A *After grinding or honing, turn blade with flat side on stone to remove the wire edge formed by sharpening on beveled side.*

Drill speed should be kept above 1,700 r.p.m., but should not exceed 5,000 r.p.m.

Rounded tools, such as gouges, require a different whetting technique. Place the convex bevel of the blade against the stone. Then, with the forefinger of the left hand steadying the blade, slide the blade from edge to edge. Use even, firm pressure. Roll the gouge just enough to take in the full curve of the blade. Gouges with an extreme curve are held at bevel angle with the index finger. Flatter gouges can be steadied with a finger on each edge.

Push the rounded edge of the gouge from side to side across the stone. When the burr appears remove it from the inside with a slip stone. Slip stones should also be used often to keep woodworking tools sharp as you work on the lathe. Some woodworkers feel the inside rubbing with the slip should be light to prevent the forming of an inside bevel. Others claim a slight inside bevel is an advantage. You should experiment with both to see which works best for you.

Cabinet scrapers are burnished, rather than sharpened. But a whetstone is needed as a part of the process. To sharpen a scraper remove the old burred edge with a file, truing the scraping edge as you file. Then smooth and further true the edge with

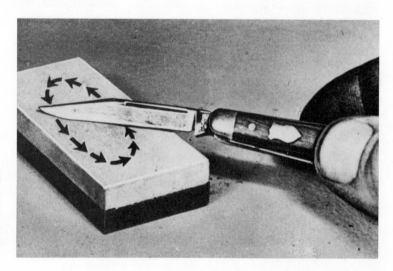

➤ *Knives and other cutting tools are sharpened by stroking the edge on the stone. A circular motion will permit full coverage of the blade edge. Do both sides an equal number of times.*

How to Keep Tools Sharp

a bench stone. Finish with a burnishing tool.

Rip and crosscut handsaws that have been dulled by normal use can be repaired by following four steps: jointing, shaping, setting and filing. The first three of these are done the same for both types of saws— the filing step, however, differs.

All teeth of a saw must be in a straight line. Low teeth don't cut and high teeth dig into the wood, causing the saw to jump or buckle. Thus, the joining step is employed to make all teeth uniform.

Place a mill file flat on the teeth with the length of the file parallel to the length of the saw. Run over the full length of the saw until the file touches the tops of all teeth. Make sure all teeth are in a staight, level line.

After jointing, teeth must be spaced and shaped as evenly as when the saw was new. If you want to get an idea how teeth looked when new, examine the butt-end of the saw. Teeth here are usually unused.

Place a slim taper file well down into the gullet between two teeth and file straight across the saw at a right angle to the blade. If teeth are of unequal size, press the file against the largest tooth until the center of the flat top made by jointing is obtained. Move to the next gullet and file until the tooth is brought to a point. Shape every tooth in this manner.

The number of teeth per inch determines the point size of the saw. For example, a saw with eight teeth per inch of blade is an 8-point saw. For the shaping and filing operation, use a 7-inch slim taper file for 4½, 5 and 6 point saws. Use a 5- or 5½-inch slim taper file for 9 and 10 point saws.

The filing operation is the actual sharpening of the tool. To file a rip saw, put the saw in a vise with the handle to your right. File each alternate tooth with a taper file. Place the file in the gullet, hold it at a right angle to the blade and file until the tooth is shaped to a point. File each second tooth

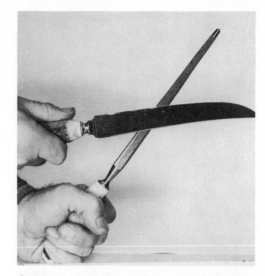

▲ Tempered steel is easiest way to keep large knives keen. Stroke the blade forward from handle, then turn the blade over and bring the stroke back to the start. Another way is to take alternate strokes on top and bottom of steel for alternate sides of the blade.

▼ Round tools, such as the gouge pictured here, are sharpened by working the bevel side to side as you draw it over the stone. Good edges depend on good sharpening habits.

◀ *Remove burr from inside with a slip stone.*

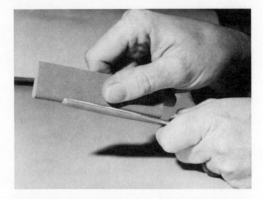

▼ *Axes and hatchets can be kept sharp by occasional honing with a round abrasive stone. Move the stone in a circular direction equally on both sides of the edge.*

in this manner. Then, turn the saw around so the handle is to your left and repeat the operation for those teeth that weren't filed.

Filing crosscut saws is done in the same way, except the file must be held at a 45° angle to the blade.

Twist drill bits should be ground in a drill holder fixture, if available, or by holding it steady by hand against the grinding wheel, which is more difficult. Grind the drill lips at an angle of 59°. Both cutting edges of the bit must make the same angle with the drill axis and must be of the same length.

Following grinding of the lips to the same angle and length, grind each heel by holding it at an angle of 12° to 15° to the grinding wheel.

Augers are sharpened with a small diameter round file. Draw the file lightly on

▼ *Auger is kept sharp by occasional strokes of a fine triangular file across the inside surface of the spurs. Take equal number of strokes on each spur for uniform cutting of chips.*

▲ *When axe edge becomes very dull or nicked, use an abrasive disk in electric drill to restore the bevel and cutting edge.*

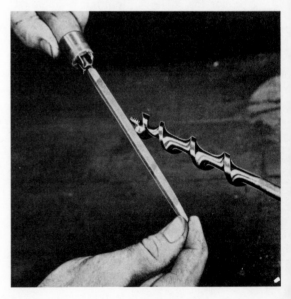

How to Keep Tools Sharp

▶ *Scissors taken apart for squaring the shearing edges with stone. Follow original bevel on both sides, grind off any burrs.*

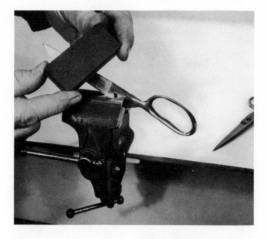

the inside of the spur, never on the outside edge. The cutter lips also can be touched up with the file, but do this on the upper edge only, taking the same amount of material from each one, so that they will cut chips of the same thickness. If the auger is bent slightly, which can be determined by rolling it on a flat wood surface, straighten by tapping with a hammer on the high side.

Sharpening scissors involves a different process as the action is that of shearing rather than cutting. A small abrasive stone is used primarily to grind away projecting burrs, and to square up the meeting edges. The essential detail is proper tightening and peening of the pivot screw. Another detail that will improve performance is cleaning of the scissors with steelwool to remove gummed or greasy residue.

See also: KNIVES AND AXES; TOOLS.

▽ *Tighten pivot screw just enough so shearing action is comfortable. Adjustment can be retained by peening the screw.*

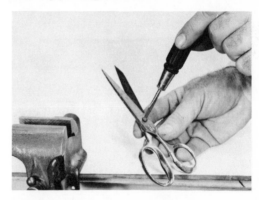

▽ *Screwdrivers need square tip so that blade will not slip out of screw slots. Hold the blade straight against stone, apply only light pressure, then square off sides of blade end.*

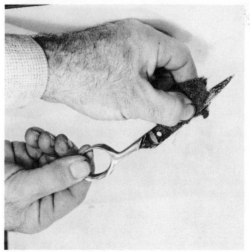

▲ *Gummed or greasy edges will retard scissor action. Clean with steel wool, then oil lightly.*

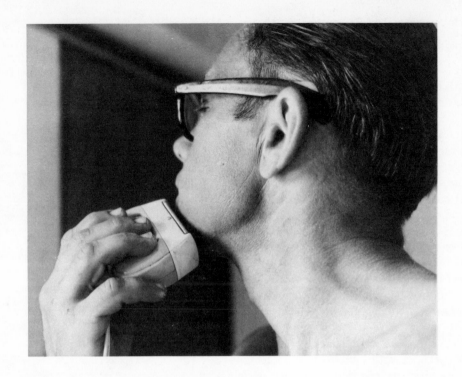

How to Sharpen an Electric Razor

**This simple task takes no skill
at all, and it will leave
your razor as sharp
as it was when it
was new—maybe sharper**

IN THE PAST you've probably thrown away those old dull electric razor heads, or else found it cheaper to buy a new razor when it started to become dull rather than replace the old head. Here's a little trick to sharpen your electric razor that really works, eliminating this tiresome problem.

Begin by taking your old razor apart, making it a point to get the cutters back in their original place. Clean them off thoroughly, washing in gasoline. Then mix a bit of fine valve compound with a cutting or penetrating oil. Rub this mixture on the cutters, slip them back in place and then rub the mixture across the head.

Next, run the razor for about one minute. Take the head off, clean it in gasoline, then remove the cutters and clean them thoroughly. Finally reassemble the razor, using a very light oil on the head to lubricate it. You'll find your razor cuts as well—if not better—than a new one. H.K.

How to Sharpen an Electric Razor

⚑ *Mix a batch of valve compound and oil.*

⚑ *Spread mixture on the cutting blade.*

⚑ *Slip the cutters back in place.*

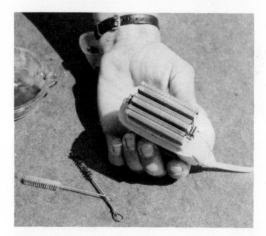

⚑ *Run electric razor for about a minute.*

➤ *Disassemble and wash head in gasoline.*

▲ Angel Wing
(Cyrtropleiva Costata Linne)

▲ Sunray Venus
(Macrocallista Nimbosa Solander)

How to Collect Sea Shells

Whether you want to join the nation's 20,000 serious collectors or merely want to enjoy the fun of finding a beautiful specimen occasionally, here's how to do it

OVER 50,000 MILES OF shoreline, 800 shoreside campgrounds and 6,000 native American sea shells are strong arguments for adding shell collecting to your list of camping activities.

No animal is as widely sought, as widely collected or as widely traded as the shellfish. At last count there were 20,000 "serious" collectors in this country and perhaps 10 times that many casual ones. If you don't number yourself among them, you're missing a great family activity.

Some people collect shells only. Others combine shells and interesting marine life. Neither is as complicated as it may seem.

Edible shellfish, such as oysters and clams, as well as "collectors specimens," like Whelks and Nassas, are available on both coasts. Public campgrounds from Acadia National Park to Bahia Honda can put east coast campers in touch with good areas from Maine to the Florida Keys. On the west coast similar opportunities range south from La Push, Washington, to Mexico.

You can gather shells from the surf, shallow water or deep water. Shallow water is the best. Beachcombing, working the surf's edge, is common but seldom productive. A few good shells may be found on the beach, especially after a storm, but live specimens are better.

When you collect from a natural habitat, you get shells in top condition with brighter, more perfect coloring. Since most species remain submerged as long as possible you must either wait for an exceptionally low tide or go in after them. You can do both. Sift the sand along tidal flats—edible clams are often gathered this way—and work the waist-deep water behind the surf.

You don't need much equipment. A swim suit or shorts, tennis shoes or rubber boots and a cloth bag or bucket are the basics. You might add a shovel and a crowbar for moving or chipping larger

⋀ Giant Atlantic Cockle
(Dinocardium Robustum Solancle)

⋀ Alphabet Cone
(Conus Spurius Atlanticus Clinsh)

⋀ Fighting Conch (Strombus Alatus Gmelin)

⋀ Scotch Bonnet (Phalium Granulatum Born)

⋀ Banded Tulip (Fasciolaria Hunteria Perry)

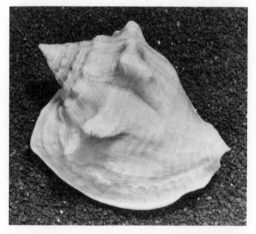

⋀ Milk Conch (Strombus Costaltus Gmelin)

REGIONAL SEA SHELL CHART

Region	Interesting and Common Species	Recommended Areas	Special Regulations
Eastern Seacoast	Edible species such as the Quahog clam plus collectors items—Cup and Saucer Shells, Striate, Atlantic, Slipper Shell and Eastern White Slipper Shell, Moon Snail, New England Neptune, Whelk, Limpet, Periwinkle, Oyster Drill, Atlantic Dogwinkle, New England Nassa, Coquina Clam.	Cape Cod shoreline is often excellent, especially in the area of the established National Seashore. The Nature Walk at Acadia National Park will give you a good idea of what the coastline can offer.	Maine's laws are complicated and often contradictory. Massachusetts has ambiguous state laws plus special township ordinances. A license is required. Usually, you are legally okay in New York if you stay clear of cultivated and leased commercial beds. In New Hampshire, out-of-state collectors can take Whelks and mussels but only residents can dig clams and oysters.
Southeast States	Edible clams, Cup and Saucer Shells, Moon Snail, several good Cowrie, Helmet Shells, American Crown Conch, Whelks, Olives, Volute, Tellin, Coquina.	There are many. Along the Carolina coast try the country off U.S. 17. In Virginia, Chesapeake Bay and the barrier reef to the east are good. Florida offers many spots. One of the most interesting is Juniper Inlet on the east coast. The Keys are the only coral reefs in the U.S.; try them. In Georgia, work the area around Sea Island.	Avoid oysters in South Carolina; in most areas legal collecting is difficult to define. Florida has no restrictions except on oysters and clams. Maryland and Virginia have restrictions on these as well. Non-residents are prohibited from collecting in the Potomac River estuary.
Gulf of Mexico	Top Shell, Turban Shell, Bleeding Tooth, Emerald Nerite, Sundial, Wentletrap, Cup and Saucer, Conch, Cowrie, Murex.	The inland coast of Florida ranks as one of the best shell collecting areas in the world. One good place there is Marco Island, south of Sarasota. There are other good areas in Louisiana and Alabama. Padre Island, in Texas, is worthwhile.	Alabama has no restrictions except against commercial dredging. Louisiana has restrictions on oysters and mussels but on no other species. Texas, with perhaps the best defined regulations prohibits collecting from commercial beds.
West Coast	Abalone, especially Red and Black, Tegula, Money, Wentletrap, Nassa (Western Fat Nassa generally) plus many species of edible oysters.	In Washington, try the coast at La Push, near the Strait of Juan de Fuca. Ocean Park is one of the top areas further south. Puget Sound offers a chance for many kinds of clams as well as collector's shells. For oysters try Hood Canal. The Oregon coast is rich in possibilities. Two good areas: a two-mile stretch of coast above Newport near the Marine Gardens and coastal sections between Port Orford and the Rogue River.	Neither Washington nor Oregon requires a license but daily bag limits are set on clams. A few areas in Puget Sound are off limits. Abalones have special regulations limiting take and size.
California	Abalone, Limpet (especially the Keyhole Limpet), Top Shell, Nassa, Slipper Shell, Tun, Fig, Moon Snail, Sand Dollar, Tellin.	In northern California, a favorite area is Shell Beach below the mouth of the Russian River. Another, the rocky headland of Bodega Bay. In the south, don't overlook the area around Morro Bay. For clams, don't miss Pismo Beach, famous of course for the Pismo Clam. Near San Diego, work the surf near La Jolla. If you have a chance to go to Baja, Mexico, try the coast between Rosarito and Ensenada. Estero Bay, south of Ensenada, is another good spot.	A sport fishing license is required for every person over 16 years of age. There are many restrictions on the manner of capture, bag limits, seasons and hours. Most of the regulations concern abalone. Check state Department of Fish and Game rules.

▲ *Crown Conch (Melongena Corona Gmelin)*

▲ *Left Handed Whelk*

▲ *Lettued Olive (Oliva Sayana Ravenel)*

▲ *Shark Eye (Polinices Duplicatus Say)*

rocks. When you are after abalone or chitons—both single-shelled, snail-like creatures that adhere to rocks—take along a knife or pry bar and a kitchen sieve.

You can hunt shells at all hours and, while daylight yields good specimens, night is more productive. Most mollusks come alive after dark. At either time, you will discover two people, working as a team, will yield the best results. One can do the heavy work, moving rocks and scooping sand and the other hold the flashlight and bag the prizes.

Whether you collect by day or night, try all such likely areas as sand bars, mud flats, rocks and crevices. Snails, small shellfish and crabs are often found beneath rocks. You can catch many small specimens by sifting mud with a sieve. Some collectors,

working on a larger scale, use homemade screens on wooden stands. Many species are seasonal and shellfish you miss once may be abundant next time around.

Check seaweed and algae carefully. Many small mollusks live on or near them. Washing the leafy sections in a bucket of salt water will dislodge specimens. When working coral, take the same care. If it is legal, break off a branch and place it in a tub of fresh water. By morning the inhabitants of the branch, mostly mollusks and worms, are on the bottom of the tub.

Some shells come from deep water. You can search these areas with skin-diving gear. Though you can use a face mask in waist-deep water. An elaborate skin-diving set-up is not really necessary. A collector working in shallow water can usually outperform a skin diver; in deep water you can gather shells by dredging.

You can make a simple dredge, 20x30x8 inches, from iron bars and fine mesh screen. Lower it over the side of your boat and drag the ocean bottom until it seems full. It is effective to about 100 feet.

A few carnivorous species can be caught with bait. Place rotten meat or fish in a sack, weight it and sink it below the surface in the evening. A rope is floated at the surface to mark the spot (an empty plastic bleach bottle makes a good float). When you retrieve the sack in the morning, carrion-eating snails with beautiful shells usually come up with it. On the east coast, you can collect mud snails such as the Eastern, New England and Variable Nassa as well as Auger Shells like the Atlantic and Concave Auger. On the west coast, you can collect the San Pedro Auger, Western Mud and Western Fat Nassa with bait.

If you like to save both the shell and its original owner, mollusks can be preserved safely in a 70 per cent alcohol solution. Do not use formalin; it weakens and destroys most shells. If you prefer to save shells only, salt water species can be killed painlessly by placing them in warm water or preservative. When the mollusk is dead, the soft parts can be removed with a pick. If you let the specimens dry for a few days many shake free of their shells. Rinse the empty shell with soapy water then let it dry in the sun until it is odorless.

Store the cleaned shells in boxes. The brittle ones should be protected with cotton or balled newspaper. In the beginning cardboard boxes will work well, but once you assemble a sizeable collection you will want more order. You might want to keep your collection in a cabinet. A good size one measures about 3½ feet tall, 3 feet deep and 30 inches wide. You can make one for a few dollars. Keep the drawers shallow, just tall enough for your largest shells.

As you organize your shells you will want to identify them. Some shells are easy to identify; others require an expert. The important features vary with the species. Coloration, for example, is of great importance with Volute and Miter shells but of little help with Olive shells. Many common species can be identified from shell books, but you will find a few which require a more penetrating analysis. When you are in doubt about a shell, check with another collector or with the curator of a good museum. There are excellent collections in New York, Washington, D.C., Philadelphia, Chicago, Los Angeles and San Francisco.

In the beginning, common names will be adequate and there is no reason to work over scientific Latin and Greek terminology but in time you will want it because it is accurate and exact. Any number of good library books can help you sort out the family, genus and species.

Atlantic, Pacific and Gulf Coast states all offer chances for many unusual, exciting shells. For a well-rounded collection you will have to work them all or trade with collectors in other areas. But in the beginning one area can supply enough shells for an impressive start.

Cape Cod is the dividing line for thousands of sea creatures. Here, water temperatures change. To the north, in the Boreal Province, are live shellfish not found farther south. And to the south, in the Carolinian Province which ends in mid-Florida, are still other species. The southern portion of Florida belongs to the tropical Caribbean Province with still other shells.

In the accompanying chart, the most common and interesting shells are listed with their common names by regions. Although common names are often regional, they are accurate. In most states, collecting is regulated by law. Some states are liberal, some are not. The more important regulations are noted along with a few of the more productive areas.

See also: CAMPING; SCUBA DIVING.

Mirror-back Georgian Wall Shelf

The mirror-back of this beautiful Chippendale-style shelf will make both sides of your prized objects visible

AN AMERICAN CHIPPENDALE chair splat inspired the flowing lines of this mahogany wall shelf that enables you to effectively display both sides of prized ceramics and antiques.

The design affords a pleasant workout for your scroll or saber saw, with a choice of three different shaping instruments, depending on how much time you want to devote to the project.

In the deluxe treatment, as shown in the photograph, the side cutouts are carried to the points and the molded edges hand-tooled in the corners. Another way is to curve the saw blade around the angles and follow with a molding cutter, thereby eliminating the hand work. The third way is to make it a plain scroll-saw job.

Kiln-dried mahogany sized to thickness is available from craftsman supply houses, or rough stock often can be purchased at your lumberyard at less cost. A thickness of 1¼-inch will give you ½-inch panels or two ⅜-inch shelves by resawing. To get the two ⅜ x 6 x 20-inch top and bottom shelves, surface the sides, joint the edges, gauge for thickness, and kerf the edges deeply with a circular saw as in the drawing. The stock can be divided with a hand or bandsaw.

Patterns for the saw-pierced parts are in the drawing. Lay out a 6 x 25-inch rectangle, divide it into 1-inch squares, and sketch the outline for the side pieces. Scraps of mahogany can be utilized to make the cresting.

Cut a ³⁄₁₆ x ⅜-inch dado in the sides for the ⅜ x 5¾ x 20-inch center shelf, then make a ¼-inch rabbet in the top and bottom shelves and sides for the back mirror.

To shape the sides, join the two pieces of ½ x 6 x 25-inch mahogany with finishing nails driven through the end waste. Bore starting holes at sharp corners of the openings and use a ³⁄₁₆-inch scroll blade to nego-

shingles: see roofs

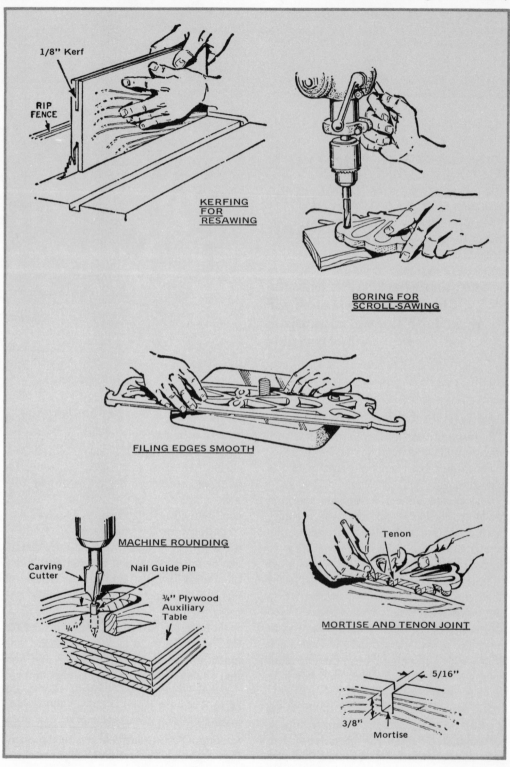

1/8" Kerf

RIP FENCE

KERFING FOR RESAWING

BORING FOR SCROLL-SAWING

FILING EDGES SMOOTH

MACHINE ROUNDING

Carving Cutter

Nail Guide Pin

¾" Plywood Auxiliary Table

¼"

Tenon

MORTISE AND TENON JOINT

5/16"

3/8"

Mortise

Mirror-back Georgian Wall Shelf

tiate all the curves in sawing. Bore large tangent holes at the ends of the loops in the sides and for the cresting detail as in the drawing. Cut the side ends after the inside sawing is smoothed wtih a fine sandpaper or with a file head held in the saw chuck.

An 8-inch wood file broken off to 5-inch length with the tang ground to fit the chuck cuts rapidly and smooth, and the edges penetrate sharp angles. A regular scroll-saw file with rounded edges or a small full-round file broken to length can get into small curves.

Machine rounding of the edges is a rapid drill-press operation, with the exact profile depending on the bit used. A small Atlas carving bit was used for the sides in the photograph. The guide pin in the drawing is a nail the same diameter as the point of the cutter, driven in and cut off ¼-inch above the table surface. Position the bit on the pin and feed the work against the rotation. Mold both faces of all scroll-sawed parts, with the exception of the rabbets, and shape the front edges of the shelves.

Smooth down any sharp edges with a fine-cut half-round machinist's file that is rolled and slid sideways as it is rocked over the edge. Cut lightly into the corners with a knife and pare away the sides to form the miters.

Before assembly, sand with 2/0 garnet paper, then 4/0, and finish with 6/0 paper. Use a plastic resin glue to assemble the unit. Insert a protective wood block under the clamp jaws, square the assembly, and nail diagonal strip across the back to make it rigid. Wipe off all excess glue with a damp cloth, so stain will take.

Mark the mortise-and-tenon joint for the cresting as in the drawing, saw the rabbets and finish by chiseling. Be sure to keep the cresting upright when gluing it in place. If necessary, clamp a board to the edge of the top shelf to prevent any forward tilt.

Round off the protruding shelf corners to meet the sides. Fill any openings with red

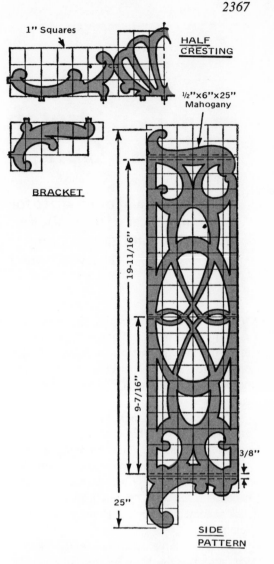

1" Squares

HALF CRESTING

½"x6"x25" Mahogany

BRACKET

19-11/16"

9-7/16"

3/8"

25"

SIDE PATTERN

mahogany paste filler, and finish with clear varnish or lacquer in a high or soft gloss.

The leaves of 1½-inch butt hinges with the barrels hacksawed off make convenient clips for installing the 19½ x 20³⁄₁₆-inch mirror. Lay the unit on a cloth or paper pad and position the mirror in the rabbets. Slip a square of thin cardboard between the clip and mirror back before tightening the ½-inch screws to prevent scratching. Use two small screw eyes for hangers.   E.M.L.

See also: CABINETS; CARVING; FINISHING, WOOD; WOODWORKING.

Four Ways You Can Stretch Your Garage

How to add more space for a bigger car or for tools, toys and garden supplies and equipment

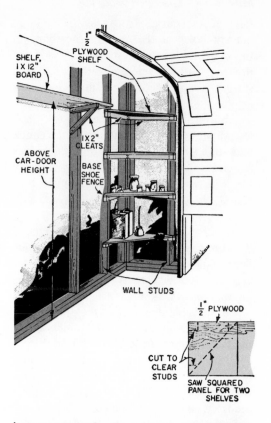

HAVE YOU TRIED opening the door of a new car in an old garage? You might make it—at least part way—if you're lucky enough to clear the bicycle, power mower or other paraphernalia stacked along the garage wall.

It's no secret that most of today's garages are so stuffed with big cars and household equipment that they are groaning at the seams. Yet trading in your car for a smaller one, or building a larger garage are both expensive solutions to the problem. Let's look at some more practical and economical solutions.

Using available space efficiently. Before you start tearing down one of your garage walls to enlarge it, or build additions, consider the height dimension of your present garage rather than just the length and width of the floor space. Getting the small stuff off the floor and on to shelves or hung up may solve your storage problem. Perforated hardboard with the various hooks available make it easy to hang up every hand-held tool for home and garden. Merely nail the perforated hardboard to the garage wall studs or 1 x 3-inch furring strips nailed to masonry garage walls.

Corner shelves will take many small items, yet not be in your way when getting into or out of your car. Make the triangular-shaped shelves of ½-inch thick, sheathing-type plywood and support them with 1 x 2-inch cleats nailed to the wall studs. Shelves above car-door height will provide 18 to 20 square feet of storage in an otherwise unused area. Large panels of ½-inch plywood placed on top of the ceiling rafters make good storage places for items like Christmas decorations that are only used once a year. Use a stepladder to gain access and do not load to over five pounds per square inch because the rafters or lower members of a trussed rafter are not designed to be load bearing, particularly in a two-car garage.

To utilize the space between the rooftop of today's lower cars and the garage roof or rafters, build in a series of hanging racks. These wide racks or shelves are ideal for screens and storm windows, a currently idle baby crib, lawn sweeper or other bulky

Four Ways You Can Stretch Your Garage

items. Use 2 x 4-inch stock for the framing and 1 x 6-inch lumber or ½-inch plywood for the shelving. A 6-foot length of 16-inch high border-type wire fencing can be used to make a garden tool rack. Bend the wire spikes, which are normally inserted into the ground, to form hooks and staple the fencing to the garage wall studs. The same wire fencing can be used to make a garden-hose rack by bending it to a semicircular shape and fastening it between the wall studs.

If reorganizing the interior of your present garage does not give you the storage space needed, the only solution is to enlarge the garage. In fact, the added convenience of being able to store garden equipment

where it is readily accessible without moving the car every time you need it is often enough of a reason for adding storage space.

Add-on, lean-to garage additions. A lean-to built against the garage is about the easiest and quickest method for increasing outdoor storage space. A walk-in lean-to can be built on the side or end, depending on how your garage is located. Be sure to check your local building code for restrictions.

When you have decided on the location and size for the lean-to, dig out the floor slab area. In hard ground, forms may not be necessary if you excavate carefully. Dig

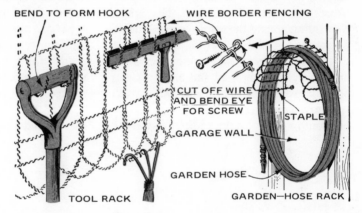

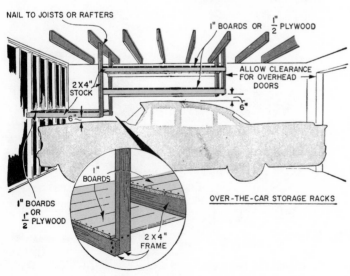

2370

it deep enough to take a 4-inch fill of gravel plus the 4-inch concrete floor. In areas where winters are cold, set tapered concrete garage piers every 6 feet along underside of outside edges of the concrete floor slab. When pouring the floor, insert ½ x 5-inch bolts around the edges of the slab for bolting down a 2 x 4-inch sill plate. Nail 2 x 4-inch studs to the plate at 24-inch spacing and to the exterior of the garage wall for the lean-to framing. For the roof, nail or lag-screw a 2 x 4-inch ledger to the side or end of the garage with room above it for 2 x 4-inch sloping rafters. Cut the rafters to slope toward the outside wall of the lean-to and apply 1-inch sheathing and roofing. Install metal flashing over the joint between the lean-to roof and the garage. New siding around the lean-to should match as closely as possible with the siding of the garage. If you can't match the siding, use an entirely different kind and make a clean break between the lean-to and the garage. A neatly painted frame lean-to can also be built onto a brick garage without disturbing the overall appearance. Caulk the vertical joint between the lean-to siding and the garage. To visually tie the new addition into an existing frame garage, paint both the same color. Wide doors in the lean-to will make it easy to get at the storage space inside. Vertical siding, nailed together with 1 x 4-inch battens inside make inexpensive doors. Where door are wide, use heavy strap hinges to support their weight.

Enlarging the width of a garage. Not only are the new cars longer and wider, but the car doors are also wider. That means more space is needed to open the car doors when in the garage. Adding a new section or moving out the side wall of your present garage is the only solution to provide the additional space needed to open the car doors when it is parked inside the garage. However, since only the central part of the wider space is needed for opening car doors, you can use the corners for storage space. By installing service doors opening to the outside, this corner storage space becomes accessible from outside the garage.

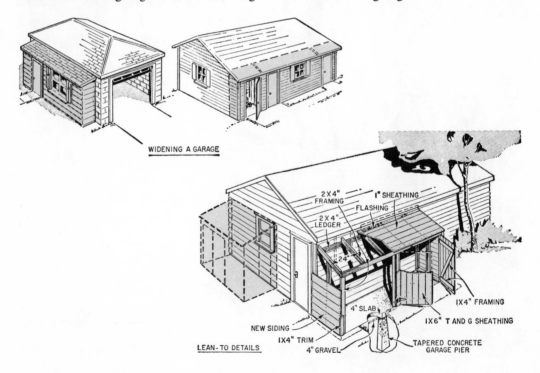

WIDENING A GARAGE

LEAN-TO DETAILS

2 X 4" FRAMING
1" SHEATHING
FLASHING
2 X 4" LEDGER
1X4" FRAMING
1X6" T AND G SHEATHING
NEW SIDING
1X4" TRIM
4" SLAB
4" GRAVEL
TAPERED CONCRETE GARAGE PIER

ADD NEW SHEATHING
AND MATCHING ROOFING

OVERLAP RAFTERS
3 FEET

36"

USE ORIGINAL
WINDOW FRAMES
AND SASH

NEW STUD WALL
OLD SIDING

NEW SLAB

REPLACE SHORT
SIDING PIECES

REMOVE OLD FRAMING
AFTER NEW WALL IS UP

ORIGINAL CORNER

ORIGINAL
CORNER

NEW CONCRETE SLAB

TAPERED CONCRETE PIERS

EXPANDING BOTH WALLS

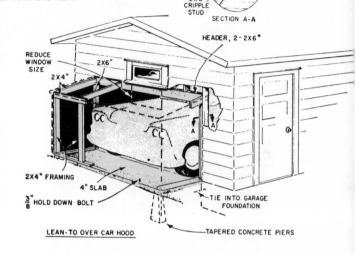

2X4" STUD

SIDING

2X6"
CRIPPLE
STUD

SECTION A-A

HEADER, 2-2X6"

REDUCE
WINDOW
SIZE

2X6"

2X4"

2X4" FRAMING

4" SLAB

3/8" HOLD DOWN BOLT

A

A

TIE INTO GARAGE
FOUNDATION

TAPERED CONCRETE PIERS

LEAN-TO OVER CAR HOOD

Start by removing the existing siding and sheathing from the wall to be widened. Dig and bury tapered concrete piers and pour a new 4-inch concrete slab floor, as for the lean-to addition. Use new 2 x 4-inch studs for the wall and extend the same roof line by nailing rafter extensions alongside existing rafters, overlapping them by 3 feet. If the existing siding is removed carefully, it can be reinstalled on the new wall. New siding in longer lengths will be needed for the ends. Remove old framing after new wall is up. If the roof is shingled, loosen the lower rows and slip the new rows of shingles under the existing shingles.

Extending the ends of a garage. If your garage is not long enough to store your new car, the additional space needed can be gained by adding to the door end, or the far end. The type of garage extension to build will depend upon the location of the garage on your lot. The simplest method of extending the useful length of your garage is to cut an opening in the far end wall and build a lean-to shelter to cover the front grille and hood of your car. Wall studs holding up the roof must be removed to open up the area. Before cutting these studs, however, install temporary 2 x 4s vertically to block up the roof. Then cut through the studs and install a double 2 x 6-inch header across the bottom ends of the cut studs. Support ends of the header with a 2 x 6-inch cripple stud that will also provide a nailing edge to attach the siding. If the header cuts

through a window, remove the lower part of the window and reinstall the upper half when the header is built in. Build the rest of the lean-to in the same way as indicated for the lean-to storage space. Remove temporary 2 x 4s after new framing is complete. If you don't care for the lean-to extension, you can extend the full end section for increased storage space or for appearance. First dig and bury tapered concrete piers and pour a 4-inch concrete slab for the new addition. Before removing the full end wall, be sure the structure is braced from all directions. In most cases the full end wall keeps the garage structure square and straight because the door end provides little bracing support. Remove all studs, sheathing and siding. At the roof line, remove the fascia. Build on a new corner at each side and splice cap plate onto the existing garage structure. Build a new wall of studs and

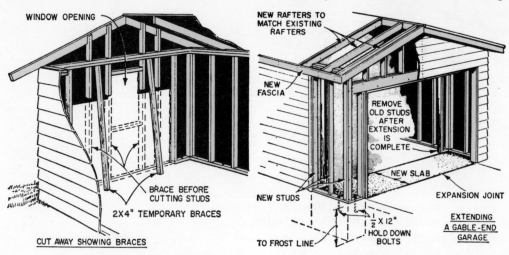

WINDOW OPENING

BRACE BEFORE
CUTTING STUDS

2X4" TEMPORARY BRACES

CUT AWAY SHOWING BRACES

NEW RAFTERS TO
MATCH EXISTING
RAFTERS

NEW
FASCIA

REMOVE
OLD STUDS
AFTER
EXTENSION
IS
COMPLETE

NEW SLAB

EXPANSION JOINT

NEW STUDS

TO FROST LINE

½ X 12"
HOLD DOWN
BOLTS

EXTENDING
A GABLE-END
GARAGE

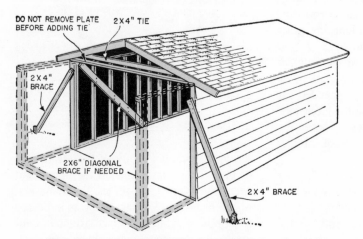

DO NOT REMOVE PLATE
BEFORE ADDING TIE

2X4" TIE

2 X 4"
BRACE

2X6" DIAGONAL
BRACE IF NEEDED

2X4" BRACE

BRACE SIDE WALLS BEFORE REMOVING ENTIRE END WALL

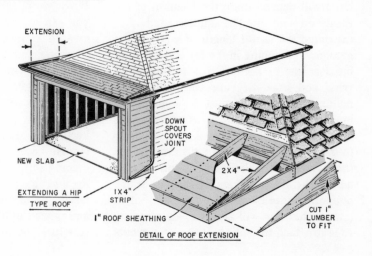

EXTENSION

DOWN
SPOUT
COVERS
JOINT

2X4"

NEW SLAB

EXTENDING A HIP
TYPE ROOF

1X4"
STRIP

1" ROOF SHEATHING

CUT 1"
LUMBER
TO FIT

DETAIL OF ROOF EXTENSION

sheathing using studs previously removed wherever possible. Cut new rafters like those on the existing garage and splice on new roof sheathing. Remove shingles along the extension joint and work new ones into each row. Install new siding to the side walls where extended and reinstall any windows or door that may have been located in the old end wall. Instead of using a stack of short siding pieces at the ends of the side walls, you may want to consider recovering the entire wall surface with cedar shakes or asbestos cement shingles. A completely new overcoat layer helps to make the garage look as if it had always been its new and larger size. A new coating of paint all over the garage will tie in the addition to the main garage.

When the garage space is part of the house and a simple end extension is not possible, the only solution left is to build out from the front or door end of the garage. This extension is more troublesome because the garage door must be relocated. However, many of the older garages that are too small for today's cars were built with swinging doors. If yours is one of these old-timers, why not extend the front end of the garage and install an easy-to-use overhead door at the same time.

To extend a simple gable-end garage first remove the fascia from around the roof and the front end siding, and the doors and sheathing. Leave the studs until the rest of the extension is completed, since they are short and probably can't be salvaged. Pour a new concrete floor as mentioned above. Build new stud walls and add one or two additional rafters to extend the roof. As long as you are extending the front end, it is often just as simple to add as much as four or six feet additional length to provide for more usable storage space. Add on roofing, wall sheathing and siding as for the other types of additions.

A variety of overhead doors, either the roll-up or fold-up type are available. Frame the door opening to the size necessary to fit the door you select, then install the door according to the instructions.

Where a hip-type roof covers an existing garage, an extension cannot be tied-in simply. Here, the simplest solution is to build on a new section and cover it with an almost flat roof. Because of the difference in roof lines, the extension should be kept as short as possible. Build stud walls and add short 2 x 4-inch rafters and sheathing. Apply built-up roof of saturated felt tucked up under shingles on existing garage. Add shingles to match existing roof or reshingle entire roof. An overhead door can be installed in most of these extensions, but make sure there is enough overhead space available for the type of door selected. The roll-up type doors usually require more overhead space than the flat one piece that swing up and into the garage over the car.

While these ideas for extending your garage are mainly applicable to frame garages, a frame extension can also be built onto a brick garage. If the garage is solid brick and/or concrete block construction, the easiest solution is to build on a completely new frame addition at the door end. A neatly painted frame building will complement a brick garage just as many houses are built with a combination of brick or masonry and frame construction. Wherever possible, leave the brick structure undisturbed and simply build on the frame portion.

When the garage is of brick veneer construction, the brick exterior can be removed and the addition built onto the frame structure. New brick veneer can then be applied around the outside of the new extension to match the existing garage. If the brick can't be matched, try using a complementary stone. Or the new extension can be covered with siding and painted just as with the solid masonry construction.   M.E.D., D.M.S.

See also: FENCE-STORAGE SHED; GARDEN TOOL SHED.

How to Build Simple Utility Shelves

Anyone with a few hand tools and average skill can make these wide, sturdy free-standing shelves.

THESE LARGE, WIDE utility shelves—so handy for many purposes in the home—are sturdy and easy to build with low-cost plywood. Simplicity is the keynote to the design; construction requires only ordinary hand tools and average skill.

Allowing for saw kerfs, lay out all parts as shown in cutting diagrams. Cut with hand or table saw, sand all mating edges and check for fit.

Mark location of 1-inch diameter holes for dowels as shown, then drill through lower three shelves with brace and bit. The top shelf will require blind holes drilled to a ⅜-inch depth.

Using glue and 6d finish nails, fasten ends to shelves. After cutting dowels to length, slip into position through holes in shelves and pre-drill for nailing. Drive nails into ends of dowels to fasten top shelf. The other shelves are held in position by nailing through shelf edges.

Set all nails and fill holes and exposed plywood edges with spackle or wood paste. Sand edges and ease corners with 3-0 paper on a soft block.

Give all surfaces a flat undercoat of paint and follow with two coats of semi-gloss enamel, sanding lightly between coats. Be sure to seal edges well.

See also: DRAWERS; FENCE-STORAGE SHED; LAUNDRY ROOMS; LUMBER; STORAGE.

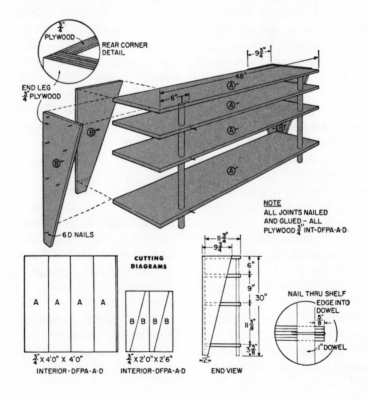

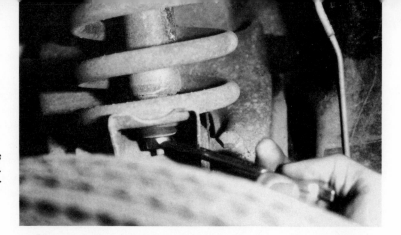

On most cars, shocks can be replaced easily. Wrench is shown on bottom shock nut.

Testing and Replacing Your Car's Shock Absorbers

Shock absorbers are easy to replace, and if your car has 20,000 miles or more on the odometer, the job probably needs to be done

TESTING YOUR CAR'S SPRINGS and shock absorbers is not difficult. With your car ready for the road but unladen with extra passengers and luggage, it should sit level on flat ground. If it does, your car's springs are okay. There should be no sagging at any of the four corners, the front end should not be lower than the rear end, and vice versa. All of this presupposes that you have never modified your car's stance with lowering blocks or oversize tires in the rear.

If you wish to make sure that your car's springs retain their factory height control specification, measure vertically from the bottom of the lower control arm, and at the extreme outer end, to the ground at each side of the front. If this measurement differs more than ¼-inch, the installation of spring spacers is recommended. No more than two spacers should be used on any spring; to exceed two spacers would allow the front coils to close up on rough roads. The rear springs, too, can be checked for height in a similar manner—by measuring vertically from the left and right ends of lowest point of the rear axle to the ground. If there is more than ¼-inch difference noted, spring spacer should again be employed. If you should find the need of spacers, take your car to a reliable spring shop where the correct spacers are available. There is the additional possibility that your springs have lost their flexibility, or some of it, and in this case either new springs are indicated or, in the case of leaf springs, redishing.

There are several ways to test shock absorbers. The best ways are a severe road test and, as a double-check, the tap-the-brakes method illustrated.

If the car drifts on hard cornering; shakes, rattles and rolls on washboard roads; and the shocks have about 20,000 miles on them; the shocks are gone. Most original equipment shocks need replacement after 12,000 to 15,000 miles.

The "hopping on the bumper" test really doesn't tell you much about your shocks. Very few modern shocks will give you a definitive answer with that test. They are designed for ride control when the car is moving down a road, and all you could simulate with the hopping-on-the-bumper test is very, very low-speed operation. Most shocks are designed for medium-to-high-speed ride control, and are virtually inactive at two mph.

Modern telescopic shocks cannot be refilled, although some British sports cars have lever shocks that are refillable.

Whether you replace worn out shocks with the equivalent of original equipment or get something better depends on how heavily you load your car and the type of driving you do.

There are low quality shocks that are worse than original equipment. Avoid these altogether. You should always replace with a premium shock. Even if your springs look good, they have lost a bit of their zest, and a premium shock will compensate for this.

If you carry heavy loads, you should install shocks with an auxiliary coil spring in the rear. These shocks are the best for the average weekend mechanic who may carry a few hundred pounds of tools and parts in his trunk.

In fact, the coil spring shock can cure a minor spring sag problem and eliminate the use of spring spacers, which have limits to their use, as explained earlier. If your car has relatively low mileage, you should consider an adjustable shock. This type is expensive but it will normally last twice as long as a conventional design. The shock permits adjustment of the compression stroke to compensate for wear within the shock. The adjustment feature is not the only reason this type of shock lasts longer. It is a superpremium design in every respect, with a nicely finished piston rod, better sealing, more sophisticated valving, etc. The adjustable shock is available with the auxiliary coil spring too.

Probably the most important thing is to make certain that you purchase the correct size for your make and model.

The most important thing about changing shock absorbers is to securely block your car so that it cannot possibly roll in either direction. Hide the ignition key and

block the end that stays on the ground. You would do well, if there are children around, to roll all the windows up on your car and then to lock all the doors to prevent any tampering with the clutch or brakes. You don't want to find yourself pinned beneath two tons of steel for want of foresight, so also use safety stands under the A-frames after you jack up the car.

Some front shock absorbers are inside of the coil springs, others are angularly displaced outboard of the front coils. Removal is simple and consists mainly of removing the top nut and lifting off the washers and rubber bushings from the top lug. The latter is either attached to the car's frame or it extends vertically through a web-like plate that is attached to the top of the coil spring. The bolt that secures the bottom of the shock absorber through the mounting plate on the lower A-frame arm is then removed. Some bottom mounting plates must themselves be removed from the lower A-frame in order to allow removal of the shock absorber. Some makes use a saucershaped washer of generous size to hold the bottom end of the shock absorber to the A-frame or the bottom of the coil spring.

Take note of the order in which washers, rubber grommets or bushings and various small parts are removed so that the same order can be retained when you install the new units. Make a rough diagram of the order to aid your memory.

To install the new shocks, first fit them in place loosely securing top ends first. In some cases the top of the shock has an integral steel ring inside of which there are rubber bushings. You should always receive new bushings with a new set of shocks. Before replacing the new shocks, squirt a bit of brake fluid on the rubber bushings to make them seat more easily. Now on the bottom end of the new shock install the mounting plate (if that web-like piece comes free upon removal or has to be removed), the bushing, the washer, the lock

Testing and Replacing Your Car's Shock Absorbers

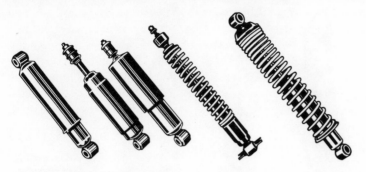

◄ *Typical replacement shock absorbers. The three at the left are conventional heavy-duty units. The two at the right are fitted with auxiliary springs. The narrower unit is for front wheels, the wider one for the rears.*

washer if any, and the locking nut—in that order—and tighten securely.

In some other cases, especially where the shock absorber is mounted inside of the coil spring, it will be necessary then to replace the bolts which hold the bottom end mounting plate against the lower A-frame arm. Once the bottom end is secured, the washers and nut are replaced on the top mounting bracket. With a torque wrench preferably, tighten the bolts.

Rear shock absorbers, generally, install much as do the front units. There are some variations depending, again, on whether the rear shocks attach on the bottom ends to a web plate mounted to the side of the leaf springs, to a bracket on the top or bottom of the leaf springs, or to a bracket on the ends of the axle housing. In a few cases the shock absorbers mount inside of the coil on rear coil spring suspensions of older cars; this is rarely found, however.

Generally, the rear shock absorbers are canted outward in order to achieve greater stability and, therefore, lugs or brackets are employed to secure the bottom ends. Most rear shock absorbers mount, at the top ends, through the steel floor of the car— the mounting bolts extend through and into the trunk compartment or, in the case of many station wagons, into the spare wheel bin beneath the rear floor. Washers, lock washers, and nuts secure the top ends and the removal of these is generally easier than to loosen the top ends of the front shocks due to more space.

The removal of any shock absorber, front or rear, is made easier if you take a few moments to inspect the means by which those used on your car are mounted. Sometimes, in order to reach the upper mountings in front, it is necessary to remove the front wheels. The same is true of the rear shock absorbers.

Try the car out over the same course on which you discovered the old shocks to be faulty. Make some quick stops and note how the new units stop the vertical jounce and rebound.

The tools you will need for replacing shocks are the open-end or box-end wrenches generally found in the kit of the average do-it-yourselfer. A large screwdriver is sometimes handy for prying loose a stubborn lug bolt once the nut is removed, and a torque wrench is desirable.   P.W.

See also: BALL JOINTS; BEARINGS; HAND TOOLS; PARTS REPLACEMENT, ENGINE.

▼ *To double-check apparently bad shocks, drive car on smooth pavement at about 10 mph. Tap the brakes repeatedly, and if this sets up a rocking motion (front end down, rear end up; then vice versa), the shocks are bad.*

How to Get Your Weapon in Shape

A poorly functioning rifle or shotgun could cost you a shot, a trophy, or an entire hunting trip. Use this simple guide to avoid the pitfalls

HUNTING, LIKE EVERYTHING ELSE, costs a lot of money these days; and the smart shooter can protect his investment by adequate testing and preparation prior to the hunt. Preventing malfunctions of your rifle and accessories in the field eliminates the need for time-wasting cures.

A rifle overhaul should include tightening of the guard screws as well as all screws of the scope rings and base. Most stocks will eventually compress between the pressure of the action and trigger guard, and scope rings and base screws have a tendency to loosen unless they have been cemented in.

You can determine, by feel alone, if the trigger pull is excessively heavy or light. It can be weighed either by spring scales or by using a can of sand string-suspended to the trigger. Ordinary kitchen or fisherman's spring scales, with an attached hook, will indicate near-accurate weight. Or two holes can be punched in a small tin can, with the attached string looped around the trigger, and sand poured into can until the firing pin is released. The can of sand is then weighed for the trigger pull weight.

Some trigger adjustments on bolt actions are simple enough for you to handle. Manufacturer's instructions or handbooks are available for adjusting trigger pulls on most bolt actions. Many authorities recommend a pull of 3½ or 4 pounds for hunting rifles.

Under most conditions the average hunter will not be hampered, consciously, by a creepy trigger. However, in long-range game shooting, a grating sear engagement precludes good holding. Any work on sear engagement should be taken to a gunsmith; it is not a job for the novice.

Proper functioning of the safety is vital, and it must hold under rough usage in actual hunting. You can check its functioning by jarring the rifle and by fast manipulation of the bolt, safety and trigger. If safety fails at any time under these tests, rifle should be corrected by a gunsmith.

Frequently, situations develop when a fast second shot is necessary to drop or finish off the game. A bolt that binds under these circumstances can prevent an effective second shot and result in actual loss of the animal. A bolt may operate smoothly enough in slow fire but develop a tendency to bind under fast handling because of an eccentric throw. Check the bolt operation under rapid fire conditions to be sure it moves smoothly in the receiver.

Cartridges, particularly if hand-loaded, should be run through the magazine, chambered and extracted. Cartridge length must permit functioning through magazine. Cases that are partially resized, or neck-sized only, should be chambered to make sure they fit. And some tight chambers will not accept all factory rounds. Consequently, all hunting cartridges—whether factory or hand-loaded, should be test chambered and extracted to prevent possible malfunction in the field.

Sighting in is a simple procedure and must be performed by the hunter himself since no two men hold and fire alike. A bench rest is best, particularly if hunting is expected to involve long range shots. However, any temporary rest will do, or you can fire from the prone position. If you're not sure about bullet impact, fire the first shots at 25 yards and adjust the sights until your

bullets group in the bullseye. Then check the impact at 100 yards and make any necessary corrections.

A zero of 100 yards is adequate for the

⋏ *The ingredients for sighting in are simple: a solid rest, a spotting scope and a rifle rest.*

⋎ *This .270 was zeroed in to print 2¹/₂ inches high at 100 yards, which adjusts it for long-range shooting.*

timber and brush habitat of the whitetail. Antelope and open-country mule deer require a bullet impact about 2½ inches high at 100 yards—provided the muzzle velocity of the load is around 3,000 fps. Your rifle should again be checked at the maximum range at which you expect to shoot. Subsequent scope adjustment may be necessary to provide a longer-range zero. But be sure to use the load—or loads—you plan to use on the hunt.

If you're mounting a new scope or switching a scope from one rifle to another, bore sighting is necessary. Cut a V notch at opposite ends of a cardboard box to hold the rifle steady. Set up a paper bull 100 yards from the table on which the cardboard box and rifle rest. With the bolt removed look through the barrel and align the bore with the bullseye; then, without moving the rifle, adjust the scope so the crosshairs quarter the bull. Then look down the barrel again to see if bore still is lined up with the bull.

This is easier and quicker if an empty, deprimed case is inserted into the chamber. The case flashhole, being smaller than the rifle bore, facilitates aligning the bore with the target.

Another method is to fire the rifle at the 25-yard target, then adjust the scope so the crosshairs coincide with the bullet hole. The scope then can be adjusted—by sighting shots—for whatever zero is needed. It's merely a question of making the crosshairs coincide with bore, then zeroing for desired range. Most scope mounts have windage adjustment in the base. Your first adjustments—if the gun is way off—should be made with the base windage screws, and the final, fine adjustments made with the dialing mechanism on the scope.

Bullets with a velocity in the .270 bracket (3,140 fps), if scope-sighted to zero at 250-275 yards, will first cross the line of sight at approximately 25 yards—hence the recommendation that your first sighting-in

shots be taken at that distance. If you're dead on at 25 yards, with cartridges in the above velocity bracket, your zero of 250-275 yards will take care of most open-country shooting.

Don't take anybody's word for it—do your own shooting at the longer ranges to be sure the zero is where you want it. Distances of 300-400 yards, however, look much longer in actuality than they do on paper. You may decide that 275 yards is an adequate—and compatible—zero.

After your rifle is zeroed, get in as much practice shooting as possible—at those ranges you expect on the hunt. This is one of the most neglected phases of hunt preparation, yet it is the most important. Shoot from all positions at various ranges, and shoot at paper targets so you'll have a ready reminder of marksmanship and improvement.

Special emphasis should be placed on the offhand position. This is the most difficult and necessitates much longer practice and conditioning.

There are various standards of gauging marksmanship. One authority says that a man who—offhand—can keep his bullets in a 6-inch circle at 100 yards is a very good shot. Sitting permits much closer holding but the rifleman who shoots well from the standing position seldom has to worry about accuracy when shooting from the much steadier "sit." The vital chest area of deer-sized game provides a near 12-inch target; so the hunter, in practice, can use such a bullseye as a standard.

The handloader can work up a reduced practice load which will lessen recoil, thus making practice less jarring. This is particularly true if rifle has a stiff recoil. For instance, a .30/338 might have much less wallop with a load of 55 grains of 4895 and a 152-grain bullet than with a hunting load using the 165- or 180-grain bullet.   D.B.

See also: HUNTING; PATTERNING, SHOTGUN; RE-LOADING; SHOTGUN.

How to Make Your Own Ammunition

If the ammunition for your weapon is in short supply, you can make your own. All you need is some equipment and a source of rounds that are fairly close to the type you require

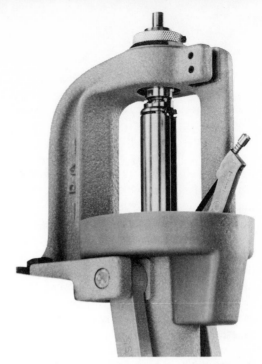

▲ *Reforming a 30-06 case to 7.65 Mauser, using a RCBS 7.65 Mauser trim die.*

THERE IS REALLY NOTHING NEW about making cases of one caliber from another. The factories have done it for generations. The old 45/70 case was necked down by Winchester to make .33, 38/56, 40/65 and other calibers. The 30/30, 25/35 and .219 Zipper were nothing more than the old 38/55 Winchester case necked down in varying degrees. In more modern times, the great .270 Winchester was produced by simply necking the 30/06 down, and the .243 and .358 Winchester rounds later came from the 7.62mm NATO case similarly treated. The fine 6mm Remington is only the .257 Roberts necked down very slightly—and that worthy cartridge derived from the 75-year-old 7mm Mauser in exactly the same manner.

So, if the factories can do it so glibly, there is no reason whatever that you can't convert plentiful 30/06 or other cases to take the place of the other calibers.

Of most modern domestic rifle calibers in production, over 90% of them can be duplicated from either 30/30, 30/06 or

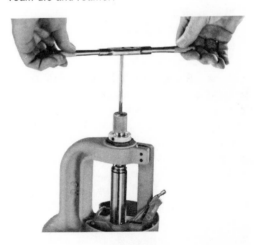

▼ *Neck reaming a case using a RCBS neck ream die and reamer.*

.300 (or .375) H & H Magnum cases. The 30/06 will handle by far the largest number of them. In short, if you have a modest supply of fired cases on hand in those calibers, the shelves of your favorite rifleshop can be completely bare of factory loads, yet you can load and shoot 90% of the modern calibers.

No great amount of equipment is required. If you have a good, heavy-duty press, a case trimmer and an assortment of dies (not necessarily in the calibers you want to make), you'll be able to get by pretty well. Generally speaking, all you'll be doing to the cases is reducing or increasing neck diameter, relocating the shoulder and changing case length.

One of simplest reforming jobs is making up .270 Winchester brass. All you need for it is a supply of military or commercial 30/06 brass and a .270 full-length resizing die. Resize those '06 cases just as if they were regular .270's. When they come out of the die they will be, except for being a few thousandths of an inch short in overall length. Since the only difference between the two calibers is in bullet diameter, the .270 die merely squeezes the '06 neck down to size. Cases made up in this way are fully equal in strength and durability to the original item. Conversely, if your need is for 30/06 cases and you have a supply of .270's available, they can just as easily serve. In this instance, the neck is expanded, rather than reduced.

There are, though, a few case forming rules you'll have to keep firmly in mind before going much farther. First, the case you intend to use must be of the same general type as the one you want to form, for example, rimmed for rimmed, belted for belted, etc.

Second, the case you intend to use must be of the same head diameter as the one you want to make. Some slight tolerance is acceptable here, in that good cases will expand as much as .015″ just ahead of the web without danger—providing pressures are kept moderate.

Third, cases to be used must be approximately the same or greater length than the one to be made up. Here, again, some leeway is allowable. Cases with fairly long necks, such as the .270, may be as much as $\frac{1}{16}$″ short without causing any trouble.

Short neck cases like the 6.5mm Remington Magnum can't tolerate any reduction in an already too short neck.

Fourth, the cases to be used must be of modern design and fairly recent manufacture. Above all, they must be originally intended for use with smokeless powders. To use 50-year-old thin-headed black powder cases for high intensity smokeless load is to invite disaster.

Last, careful attention must be paid to the loading of such reformed cases to insure that they are not used with ultra-hot loads—remember, you reform cases to be able to shoot a gun that couldn't be used otherwise. Be happy with that advantage alone and don't try to strain things.

The 7x57 Mauser case makes a typical reforming job. You've got a nice 7mm and you want to shoot it, but the local hardware store doesn't have any new ammunition to fit it. Of course, you'll first need reloading dies in that caliber, but you probably already have them. And, of course, you have your press and other paraphernalia for the job.

Next you need a basic case that can be reworked to fit the 7mm chamber. Look first for a common and inexpensive case for the job. There are a number of books that contain extensive listing of cast dimensions that will enable you to search out a substitute in short order. However, a summary of this listing is shown with the accompanying chart. Looking through it you'll find that while there are plenty of other cases with the same head diameter as the 7mm, the old 30/06 is plentiful. It is also a modern case meant for high pressures, and it is appreciably longer than the 7mm, therefore allowing you to make full length cases.

Depending upon the lot of '06 brass that you have for the job, it may be possible to squeeze it down to size in one pass through the 7mm resizing die. But it may not if the brass is either harder or softer than what your particular die and press will handle. Good advice is to assume that it will not and start with an intermediate sizing operation. Any caliber resizing die that lies somewhere between 7mm and '06 in size and shape will do for the first step. The .308 Winchester makes an excellent intermediate die for almost any reforming work to be done on the 30/06 case.

Place a good 7mm case in the shell holder of your press and run it to the top of its stroke. Screw the .308 die (minus decapping stem) into the press until it contacts the 7mm case lightly, then lock it into place. Running the '06 cases into this die will reduce them enough to enter easily into the 7mm die. Of course, you will have remembered to clean and lubricate the cases first.

With the intermediate reduction of the '06 cases accomplished you can now set up the 7mm die in the press, also minus its decapping stem. Adjust the die just as you

would if you were resizing standard factory 7mm cases. Run the '06 cases into this die. Do each case with a single, smooth, fast stroke of the press handle. Once the brass starts moving, it's best to finish the job. If you stop in mid-stroke, it's just that much more work to get brass flowing again.

When you pull the '06 cases out of the die they will be 7x57mm Mauser cases with necks that are far too long. The excess must be removed. You may have a case trimmer around, but cutting off nearly ⅜-inches of brass with it will be an awfully slow process. An inexpensive tubing cutter of the type sold in most department and hardware stores does the job more quickly and easily. Merely mark the cases lightly with a file at a point about $\frac{1}{32}$-inch longer than factory 7mm cases. With the tubing cutter, cut off at the mark.

A case trimmer will now come in handy to trim the case back to *exactly* 7mm length. However, if you don't have one, simply take

Caliber	Type	Head Diameter	Length	Operations Required
.22-250	rimless	.469″	1.91″	Reduce progressively, trim, ream
.243 Win.	rimless	.470″	2.045″	Size .308, trim, resize .243, ream
.244 Rem. (6mm Rem.)	rimless	.470″	2.23″	Size 7mm, trim, resize 6mm, ream
.250-3000	rimless	.468″	1.91″	Make .243, trim, resize .250, ream
.257 Robts.	rimless	.471″	2.23″	Make 7mm, resize .257
.270 Win.	rimless	.469″	2.54″	Size full length .270
.280 Rem.	rimless	.468″	2.54″	Size full length .280, fire form
7x57mm	rimless	.472″	2.23″	Size .270, size 7mm, trim
.308 Win. (7.62mm NATO)	rimless	.468″	2.01″	Size .308 full length, trim
.300 Sav.	rimless	.470″	1.87″	Size .300 full length, trim
7.65mm Mauser	rimless	.468″	2.09″	Size 7.65mm full length, trim
7.7mm Jap.	rimless	.474″	2.28″	Size 7.7mm full length, trim
8mm Mauser	rimless	.470	2.23″	Size 8mm, full length, trim
.358 Win.	rimless	.469″	2.01″	Size .358 full length, trim

CASE DIMENSIONS

NOTE: Basic case from which the above may be formed is .30-06 rimless, .469″ head diameter, 2.5″ length.

a smooth, double-cut six- or eight-inch file and carefully dress off that last $\frac{1}{32}$-inch of extra brass. At the same time, take care to keep the case mouth neat and square. Chamfer the mouth inside and out just as you would any case for its first reloading.

Now, place the decapping stem and expander plug back in your 7mm die and set it up in the press for normal full length resizing. Wipe the cases clean and relubricate sparingly if needed. Resize full length. They are now genuine 7x57mm cases, no matter what the headstamp might say. If they were original military '06 cases, they need only removal of the primer crimp and they'll be ready to load. There is, however, one more refinement that's well to add if you want the cases to last as long as possible.

The brass will have "work-hardened" from the reforming process. Also, the portion of the '06 case body that now forms the 7mm neck was originally harder than case necks should really be. All this combines to create a condition that will cause the necks to split after only a few loads and consequent resizings. In fact, some lots of reformed military brass will split from internal stresses after a few months, even if they are never fired.

The above condition can be corrected by annealing the necks. This must be done before priming, or the heat involved just might set a primer off. Heating the brass of the neck above a certain critical temperature, then plunging it into cold water, relieves the stresses and leaves the brass soft and malleable. The simplest method of accomplishing this is to heat the necks quickly to the point where they just begin to change color, while standing on their heads in about an inch of cold water. When the neck begins to change color, the case is simply knocked over into the water. A small propane torch similar to the Bernz-O-Matic provides excellent heat for this.

The heat must not be allowed to flow into the head of the case. If it does, then the head will also be softened to the point where it will not stand the pressures of firing. Such a soft head combined with a hot load can completely demolish the best rifle and injure the shooter. So long as heat is applied quickly, and the case knocked over into the water just as soon as the neck begins to change color, the heads will remain cool. To make absolutely certain that heads do not get too hot, some handloaders hold the case in their fingers while playing the flame over the neck. If the head becomes hot to hold, they immediately drop it into the water, knowing that it has not yet gotten hot enough to be damaged. Better to leave the neck a little hard than spoil a case.

A number of references have stated that case necks should be heated until they turn red in order to be properly annealed. This is not so. A temperature as low as 400 degrees will relieve all the stresses and leave the brass soft enough to work properly. In fact, when heated red, the chances are pretty good the case neck is in worse shape than before annealing. Heat only until change in color is seen—the neck will turn brown or blue and the color will be seen to advance toward the shoulder. When that happens, dunk it quickly.

The foregoing procedures will produce a case that is just as good for reloading as any you can buy. Normally, though, such a case will have somewhat less internal capacity than those that come from the factory. For this reason you should always work up separate loads for reformed cases. That difference could easily raise pressures to the danger point if a near-maximum load in factory cases was used in reformed brass.

All these procedures will suffice to make cases in a great many calibers. Normally, if the amount of neck diameter reduction is small, or if the neck is increased in diameter, no further treatment of the neck is required. However, when necks are reduced a large amount, the walls thicken to the point where the case will not enter the chamber with a bullet in place. When that happens, the necks must be reamed to remove the excess brass.

If only a very slight amount need be removed, it can sometimes be accomplished from the outside by use of steel wool or sandpaper. This is a slow process, and if more than a handful of cases is to be processed, you'll do better with a reamer. If a lathe is handy, though, you can simply press the cases on to a bullet-diameter mandrel and turn excess off the outside.

One of the simplest and most economical reamers on the market is the Forster-Appelt. It consists merely of small reamers to be used in that firm's standard case trimmer. This type of tool is entirely adequate for normal use. However, if you must have maximum concentricity and uniformity of neck thickness, then the RCBS line neck reamer is the tool to get. It admits of no error, even if you don't understand the operation.

Usually, cases can be reduced from .30 caliber to as small as 6.5mm without any need for neck reaming. More reduction than that will probably require it. In making 22/250 cases from '06 brass, a great deal of excess brass must be removed. Reaming also becomes necessary quite often when the neck of the new caliber falls back along what was once the body of the case. Case walls get thicker toward the head, accounting for this.

▲ *An RCBS rock chucker press.*

The foregoing methods will serve for 80% or more of your needs in the event of a severe shortage of factory loaded ammunition. They will make a dozen or more calibers from 30/06, another dozen or better from belted magnums, and a few from 30/30 brass. They will also serve to make quite a number of foreign and obsolete calibers from assorted, more plentiful calibers. There are, of course, other more difficult forming operations that can be used to make old black powder cases and some of the more exotic foreign ammunitions, but they aren't necessary for most hunting rifles.

Most important, if you just keep a few hundred fired basic cases on hand, along with plenty of powder and primers, you'll always be able to prepare ammunition to shoot, no matter how little is to be bought across the counter.

See also: HUNTING; RELOADING.

▼ *Filing off top of a case in RCBS trim die.*

Improve Your Marksmanship with a Small Shooting Range

If you have no elaborate shooting range available, you can set one up yourself where you can practice safely either indoors or out

MOST OF THE PROBLEMS in backyard ranges are safety questions of distances, calibers and backstops.

If you use .22 rimfire rifles or moderately-loaded pistols and do not have a regular place to shoot, your best investment is a steel bullet trap which can be loaded into a car and set up any place it's needed. Some weigh about 45 pounds and can stop anything up to hot pistol loads.

Keeping the trap low to the ground simplifies safety precautions and has no appreciable effect on your score at 25 yards or more. If the earth is soft, a bullet that near-misses the trap will be stopped very quickly. Even if it struck a rock it wouldn't go far if you have a suitable backstop. A hillside or bank is best; a big unpopulated area of heavy vegetation is second choice.

If it is to be left near the shooting site, a trap can be mounted in wheel-barrow style.

Ideas for homemade bullet traps include a couple of cardboard boxes filled with sheets of paper or cardboard and a wooden box filled with dry sand or earth that includes a rubber diaphragm at the target end to keep sand from sifting through bullet holes. Both of these traps are for limited use. A makeship stop can also be made from a section of log with the target placed on the end. It takes a lot of shooting to chew out enough wood so that it will have to be replaced. One can use such an arrangement in a 25-foot basement range for .22 shorts.

In selecting a backstop, consider the cumulative effect of much firing. For example, concrete walls will not always hold up. With some walls, it takes only a few shots to chip the concrete away or even break through.

Nevertheless, it doesn't take much concrete to stop a single lead bullet of moderate velocity.

For pistol and smallbore ranges, slanted boiler plate makes satisfactory backstops. The indoor range can be built so the backstop is folded down when not in use.

There are ways to lessen the noise. Consider an oil drum with both ends cut out, lined with sound-absorbent material. It is highly efficient for pistol shooting, being located so the muzzle is within the drum. It has shortcomings for use with rifles as position shooting requires so much variation in muzzle height. Several drums mounted end to end can be a safety measure.

◄ *This portable target holder can be made in minutes and dismantled in seconds. The frame is made of pipe and can be lifted out of rungs which hold it to short boards.*

▼ *This setup for casual trap-shooting can be made with an inexpensive trap and a few concrete blocks. Operator is standing in pit. Even "official" targets may be thrown.*

Another simple sound absorber is a dozen or more auto tires mounted together on a wooden rack with the shooter firing through the tunnel. Even less noise will escape if a plywood bulkhead is installed at the firing end, leaving a small opening to shoot through.

Indoor ranges can be silenced to a surprising degree, if firing points are separated by soundproofed walls.

Most home ranges are intended for only one or two firing points but simplified ranges are often employed for elementary instruction; and judiciously constructed barriers about the firing points can make it almost impossible for an inexperienced shooter to point his gun so it will do any harm to others.

For instruction in prone shooting, some ranges use a barrier that prevents the muzzle from being raised much above the target.

A pistol range can be completely enclosed on high, level ground with simple

► *A homemade bullet stop is ideal for casual use. Simply place newspapers or magazines in cardboard boxes and tape the target onto the front of bullet stop.*

▲ *This equipment, plus suitable location, is all that is needed for night practice. Shielded gas lantern illuminates target. Bullet trap stops .22 rimfires.*

▼ *This is an easy to make rig for a miniature running deer target. The bullseye is moved along trolley lines by fishing reels which can be set on a post behind the shooter. Partner operates reels and keeps score.*

construction. A pit is dug for the firing point so that the shooter's firing arm would be somewhat below ground level. Then a ditch is dug to where the target is installed in another pit. Firing is through the ditch, which is covered with boiler plate or other bullet-proof material.

Except in metropolitan communities there are usually practical locations that are never used. Hilly country means natural range sites. About all you have to do is acquire use of the land and set up the targets. You should check on the hill you're firing into. If it's rocky you will want to be certain the area where the bullets actually go has a good covering of earth or sand to avoid ricochets. Don't shoot at a flat, stone bank.   C.F.W.

See also: HUNTING; PATTERNING, SHOTGUN; RE-LOADING; SHOTGUN.

▲ *Construction of a bench rest is simple. This triangular set grew quickly from scrap lumber and pieces of discarded telephone pole. Poles are set into ground for steadiness at 100 yard ranges.*

➤ *This neat and well-kept police pistol range was set up at moderate cost as a community project. Most of the larger police departments already have ranges and are willing to cooperate with clubs or reliable individuals. If your police don't have a range, several groups may band together to build one.*

All about Trapshooting

The ABC's of shooting clay pigeons, including the sport's origin and development, fundamental principles, equipment and ammunition

TRAPSHOOTING TRACES ITS ORIGINS back to England in the first quarter of the last century when a group of country squires devised the idea of augmenting their field shooting by putting live pigeons under a row of old beaver hats to which pieces of string were tied. At the command of "pull," an attendant jerked one of the strings, toppling the hat and releasing the bird. A shooter, stationed at a decorous distance behind the row of hats, attempted to hit the flying bird with his muzzle loading scattergun.

In due course, the top hats gave way to small iron traps which collapsed at the jerk of the string to release the bird—hence the name "trap." The game soon spread to this country and became very popular.

By the end of the 19th century, however, groups such as the Society for the Prevention of Cruelty to Animals began to make their voices heard in condemnation of this sport. These organizations took a dim view of the wholesale slaughter of pigeons involved—and, to a large degree, popular sentiment agreed. Historically, we have

been a nation of sportsmen and the traditions of sport require that game have a fair chance. As a result, while live birds are still held in some parts of this country and abroad, modern trapshooting involves the use of inanimate clay targets.

Artificial targets date back to the 1860's when a machine was devised to pitch glass balls through the air in simulation of the flight of live birds. Even though these balls were filled with feathers, to provide a realistic touch when they were hit by a shot charge, they were a poor substitute, in the eyes of the shooters of the day, for hitting a real bird.

By the 1880's however, a man named George Ligowski had devised something approximating modern clay pigeons. Ligowski's inspiration came from watching small boys skimming clam shells over the water. While his early targets were too fragile and his spring-operated traps for throwing them were rather crude, his idea was the forerunner of modern targets and traps. Better inanimate birds, made of pitch, plaster of Paris and sand, were later

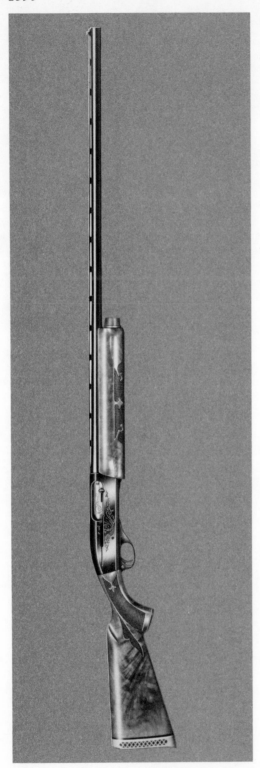

devised, along with more sophisticated devices for getting them air-borne. In due course specifications for the targets evolved to today's standards which are: diameter 4¼ inches; total height 1$\frac{1}{16}$ inches; height from rim $\frac{15}{32}$ of an inch; and weight ¾ ounce. Modern targets must be strong enough to withstand the shock of being launched from a spring-operated trap at speeds close to 70 miles per hour, yet fragile enough to break when hit by only three or four pellets of number 7½ shot at 40 yards.

By the early days of this century, trapshooting had developed into essentially its present state. Basically there are three forms of the game: 16-yard shooting, handicap shooting and doubles. All three are shot over the same basic field.

A trap field has five shooting stations, located three yards apart, set on a semicircle 16 yards behind a trap house, a low shed-like structure in which an electrically actuated, spring-operated mechanical trap for throwing the birds is located. Additional shooting stations are located on walkways extending from the 16-yard posts, at intervals of a yard, back to 27 yards. Targets are thrown from the trap at the call of "pull" by each shooter. They fly at varying horizontal angles, but are always going away from the shooter. Vertical angles are constant and the targets, starting out at a rise, gradually fall away, flying a total distance of about 60 to 70 yards.

In 16-yard shooting, five scattergunners line up, one at each post. Contestants shoot in turn until each has fired at five targets from his initial position. The shooters repeat this procedure, moving to the next station, until all have fired at five targets from each position. Thus a complete round consists of 25 targets.

In handicap shooting, the shooters, based

◄ *Autoloading trap gun showing 34-inch barrel.*

All about Trapshooting

on known ability from past performance, shoot from varying yardages. Top-flight competitors shoot from 25, 26 or even 27 yards, while those with lower averages are closer to the trap. The course of fire for handicap targets is otherwise identical to that for 16-yard shooting.

In doubles, shooting is done from the 16-yard posts but two targets come out of the house simultaneously on different angles. Skilled doubles shooters generally shoot first at the bird flying nearest to straightaway, and then go after the angled target. Top flight trapshooters are generally agreed that doubles is by far the toughest game.

The fundamental principles of the sport of trapshooting, whether targets involved are 16-yard, handicap or doubles, are fairly simple. The shooter is allowed to mount his gun with his cheek firm on the comb of the stock and his eyes looking down the barrel—in a completely "ready" position—before he calls for the bird. The target, which is released by an electrical device,

⋏ *On the firing line at 16-yard station.*

⋎ *Cutaway drawing shows plastic trap load utilizing plastic wad column to protect shot.*

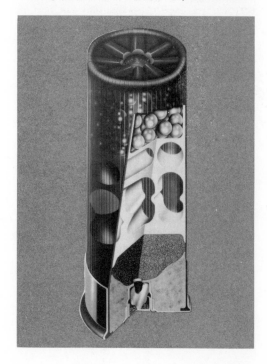

flies out almost simultaneously with the call of "pull." The shooter swings his gun along the path of flight of the target until the muzzle passes the bird, at which point he pulls the trigger. He continues his swing in a smooth, follow-through motion after he has touched off the shot, just as a golfer follows through after hitting the ball. Since target angles may vary from a complete straightaway to an angle of 25 degrees on either side of station number 3 (the center post on the field), it's clear that some shots require more "lead" than others. This is particularly true when shooting is done from handicap yardages.

The lead problem can be described with the use of two analogies. The first is the football quarterback throwing a pass to an end streaking down the field. If the end is to catch the ball, the quarterback obviously must throw it to the point where the receiver is going to be when he catches it (not where he is at the instant of throwing). One would doubt very much, however, if any topflight quarterbacks ever say to themselves, "I must throw the ball ten feet in front of where my teammate is right now, because that's where he'll be when he catches it." Rather, they estimate the situation by eye and instinctively throw to the right spot, based on experience.

The second analogy deals with a man in his backyard with a garden hose. Suppose that he wants to spray the stream of water on a dog running across the lawn. Here again, he must, obviously, point the stream ahead of the animal to hit him. The greater the angle at which the dog is running, the further ahead the man must point the nozzle. The best way that he can achieve his objective is to swing the stream of water along the path of flight of the dog, catching up with and passing the animal. If the nozzle is swung with a continuous motion, with a follow through, the water will hit the dog, building in the "lead" automatically.

Applied to clay target shooting, this sys-

tem is called the "swing and follow through" method. By swinging the gun along the path of flight of the target, pulling the trigger as the target is passed, and continuing the swing in a smooth follow through motion, the shooter is unconsciously computing the lead necessary to register a hit. He swings faster, and builds in more lead, for a quartering target than for a straightaway. Actually the distance that the gun moves, between the time the brain says "pull the trigger," the message reaches the finger, the finger does its work, and the firing pin is released *is* the lead.

While diagrams showing the amount of lead necessary for various angle targets are helpful in visualizing the situation, the key to the whole problem of hitting flying targets is "swing and follow through." Most experienced shooters will agree that the principal reason for misses is stopping the gun swing and shooting behind the target.

It is also important for new shooters to remember that a shotgun is pointed in much the same way as the garden hose in our earlier analogy, not aimed like a rifle. Many a tyro misses because he tends to wait until he has everything lined up just so, at which point the target is beyond effective range of his gun.

Many self-taught shooters violate some of the basic rules of good form and, to a degree, get away with it. In spite of their bad habits, they have learned to "groove" their swings and to break a fair number of targets. If these people had learned the fundamentals, or would take the effort to do so now, they could improve their scores a great deal.

The logical place to start in describing shooting form is with stance. The key to proper stance is to be in a relaxed position which will allow the shooter to swing his gun in whatever direction the target may fly. The knees should be slightly bent, and the shooter should be leaning in the direction in which he is going to shoot. The feet

ARC of TARGET FLIGHT

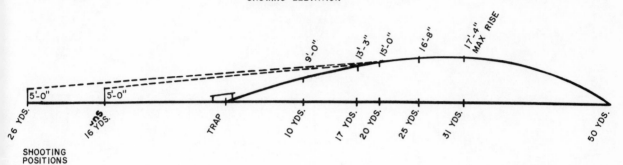

ARC OF TARGET FLIGHT
SHOWING ELEVATION

SCALE: 1" = 30'-0"

Profile view of straightaway target flight showing
relationship of shooter to target at 16 and 26 yardage marks. Also
at average "breaking points" of 17; 20; and 25 yards along
bird's course. Apex of flight is at approximately 31 yards.

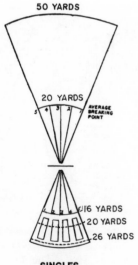

**SINGLES
CHART NO. 1**

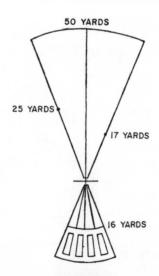

**DOUBLES
CHART NO. 1**

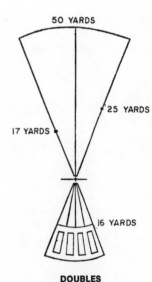

**DOUBLES
CHART NO. 2**

Singles Chart #1 shows five shooting positions
with five angles of normal target flight spaced an
equal distance (11 degrees apart). Lines have been
extended from each of five shooting positions to
indicate the straightaway target from each post. For
charting purposes these straightaway targets from
each shooting position have been given the same
number as the shooting post.

Doubles Chart #1 shows the #1 target
(right angle) at 17-yards rise, and the #5 target
(left angle) at 25-yards. As Doubles are thrown at
known angles, from a stationary trap, both targets
are shown at 22 degrees off center.

Doubles Chart #2 shows the #5 target
(left angle) at 17-yards rise, and the #1 target
(right angle) at 25-yards.

SINGLES

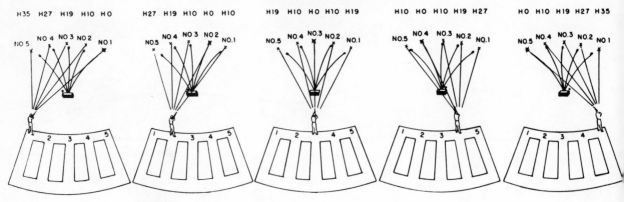

LEGEND
. HOLD MUZZLE AT THIS POINT AT CALL OF PULL
o TARGET IN FLIGHT
X SIGHT PICTURE (RELATIONSHIP OF GUN MUZZLE TO TARGET WHEN TRIGGER IS PULLED)
H HORIZONTAL LEAD IN INCHES

16 YARD SINGLES

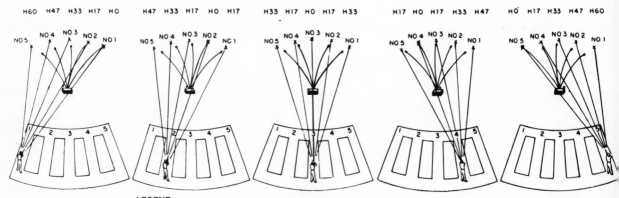

LEGEND
. HOLD MUZZLE AT THIS POINT AT CALL OF PULL
o TARGET IN FLIGHT
X SIGHT PICTURE (RELATIONSHIP OF GUN MUZZLE TO TARGET WHEN TRIGGER IS PULLED)
H HORIZONTAL LEAD IN INCHES

26 YARD HANDICAP

should be fairly close together so that weight can be changed from one to the other, pivoting the body as the gun is swung. A right-handed shooter should have his left foot advanced while the southpaw should be in the reverse position. The upper part of the body should be on an angle with the shooting shoulder of approximately 45 degrees from a line parallel with the rear of the trap house.

In trapshooting, the shooter is allowed to have the gun mounted to his shoulder in

All about Trapshooting

DOUBLES

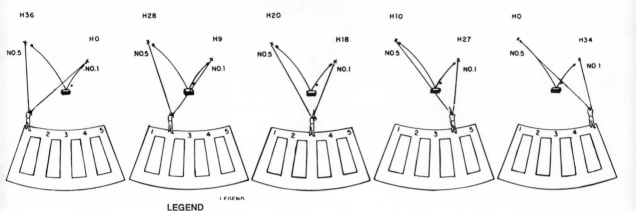

LEGEND
. POINT MUZZLE TO FAVOR TARGET YOU WILL TAKE FIRST.
o TARGETS IN FLIGHT
X IDEAL SIGHT PICTURE WHEN RIGHT ANGLE IS TAKEN FIRST.
H HORIZONTAL LEAD IN INCHES

DOUBLES RIGHT FIRST

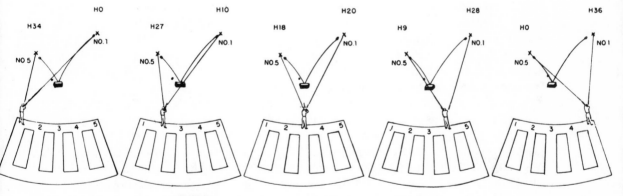

LEGEND
. POINT MUZZLE TO FAVOR TARGET YOU WILL TAKE FIRST.
o TARGETS IN FLIGHT
X IDEAL SIGHT PICTURE WHEN LEFT ANGLE IS TAKEN FIRST.
H HORIZONTAL LEAD IN INCHES

DOUBLES LEFT FIRST

shooting position when he calls for the bird. One common mistake made by beginners is putting the gun to the shoulder and then bringing the head down so that the face is against the stock. This procedure causes trouble for two reasons.

In the first place, in bringing the face down to the stock the head is apt to be tilted. This puts the eyes on an angle, making it virtually impossible to see the target properly in relation to the top of the barrel. In the second place, the head usually is not all the way down on the stock with the result that the shooter sees too much barrel. The correct procedure is to bring the gun up to the face without bending the head or neck. Shoulder position can then be adjusted.

A common error made by new shooters is shutting or squinting one eye when pointing a shotgun. Experts condemn this process, except for those whose master eye is opposite from their dominant hand. Closing one eye narrows the field of vision and makes judging distances almost impossible. With both eyes open, the shooter has depth perception and can generally outperform the squinter.

While almost any 12 gauge shotgun with a full or modified choke barrel can be used at trap, specialized muskets are available.

Pump actions, autoloaders, over-and-under doubles, side-by-side doubles and single-shot guns are all used. Obviously a double or a repeater is necessary for doubles shooting.

Since all trapshooting is done with 12 gauge shotguns, specialized trap guns, of whatever action style, are all 12 bore. The main differences between a field grade scattergun and one designed for trap are in the stock dimensions and the barrel. Trap stocks are much straighter than standard because a straight stock makes it easier to mount the gun comfortably for targets that are all "going away" at a constant vertical angle. In addition, stocks are generally fitted with a rubber recoil pad, which not only eases recoil effect on the shoulder in long races but helps to prevent the butt from slipping from the shoulder.

Barrels are usually 28 or more inches long and are fitted with ventilated ribs. Barrels of this length give a better sighting plane for more accurate pointing. Ventilated ribs also improve the sighting plane, giving the shooter an even surface the entire length of the barrel.

Trap guns are generally full choke al-though some shooters use tight-shooting, modified barrels. A full choke gun is designed to put 70 per cent or more of the shot in a 30-inch circle at 40 yards. Since the average distance at which trap targets are broken is about 40 yards from the gun, a tight pattern at this distance is necessary.

When an autoloading shotgun is used for trap, it should be fitted with a deflector to prevent ejected shells from flying into the face of the shooter on the next station. All standard autoloaders made in this country for trapshooting are so equipped.

The rules of trapshooting state that the maximum load permitted in competition may have no more than 3 drams equivalent of powder and no more than 1⅛ ounces of shot. The largest shot size permitted is 7½. The major ammunition companies manufacture loads, conforming to these specifications, that are specially designed for trapshooting. Typical are the new plastic trap loads. These shells utilize a special one-piece plastic wad column which protects the shot from deformation as it goes down the barrel and insures tighter patterns at the target.

The governing body for organized trapshooting in this country is the Amateur Trapshooting Association with headquarters in Vandalia, Ohio. Registered shoots are conducted all over the country under ATA auspices. These include state and regional championships as well as local club shoots. The "World Series" of trapshooting, the "Grand American," is held every summer on the ATA's home grounds at Vandalia. In the main event, the Grand American Handicap, more than 2,000 contestants test their skill for prizes that run into thousands of dollars.

Whether a shooter's objective is topflight competition in registered competition or just an afternoon's fun at the local club, trapshooting can provide lots of thrills and good sport.   T.M.C.

See also: HUNTING; RELOADING; SHOTGUN.

All about Skeet Shooting

The history, principles and practice of this relatively modern and more elaborate form of trapshooting

THE ORIGINS OF SKEET SHOOTING date back to about 1915 when a group of sportsmen decided to try to devise a clay target game that offered shooting situations more closely approximating those encountered in upland game hunting.

Their first attempt was a game called "clock shooting" in which shooting posts were located on the perimeter of a circle around a standard trap. The various stations offered shots at targets from all angles; outgoing, incoming, crossing and quartering.

In time the game was refined to its present form by installation of two traps which face each other—one in a "high" house and the other in a "low" house. Seven shooting stations are equally spaced

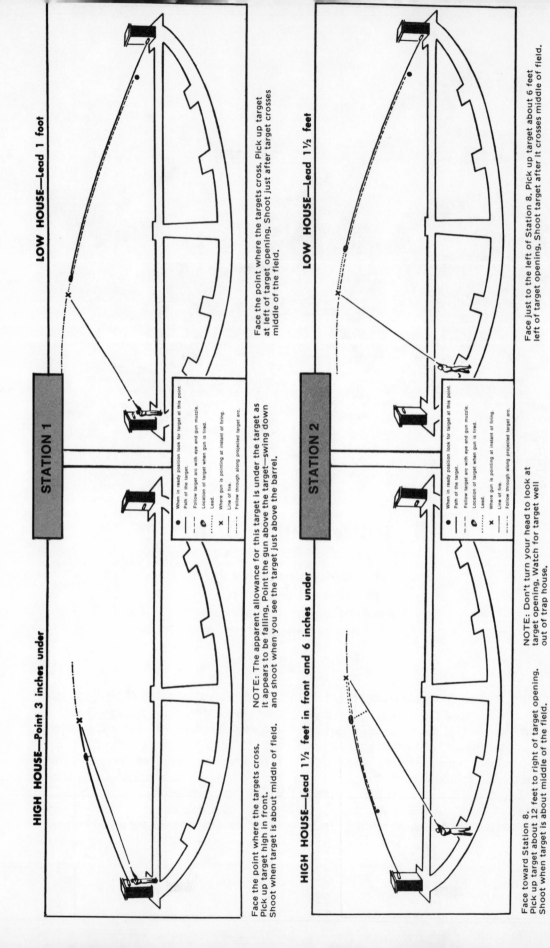

LOW HOUSE—Lead 1 foot

STATION 1

HIGH HOUSE—Point 3 inches under

LOW HOUSE—Lead 1½ feet

STATION 2

HIGH HOUSE—Lead 1½ feet in front and 6 inches under

Legend:
- ● When in ready position look for target at this point.
- —— Path of the target.
- –––– Follow target arc with eye and gun muzzle.
- ◖ Location of target when gun is fired.
- ×······ Lead.
- × Where gun is pointing at instant of firing.
- —— Line of fire.
- ––·–– Follow through along projected target arc.

Face the point where the targets cross. Pick up target at left of target opening. Shoot just after target crosses middle of the field.

NOTE: The apparent allowance for this target is under the target as it appears to be falling. Point the gun above the target—swing down and shoot when you see the target just above the barrel.

Face the point where the targets cross. Pick up target high in front. Shoot when target is about middle of field.

Face just to the left of Station 8. Pick up target about 6 feet left of target opening. Shoot target after it crosses middle of field.

Face toward Station 8. Pick up target about 12 feet to right of target opening. Shoot when target is about middle of the field.

NOTE: Don't turn your head to look at target opening. Watch for target well out of trap house.

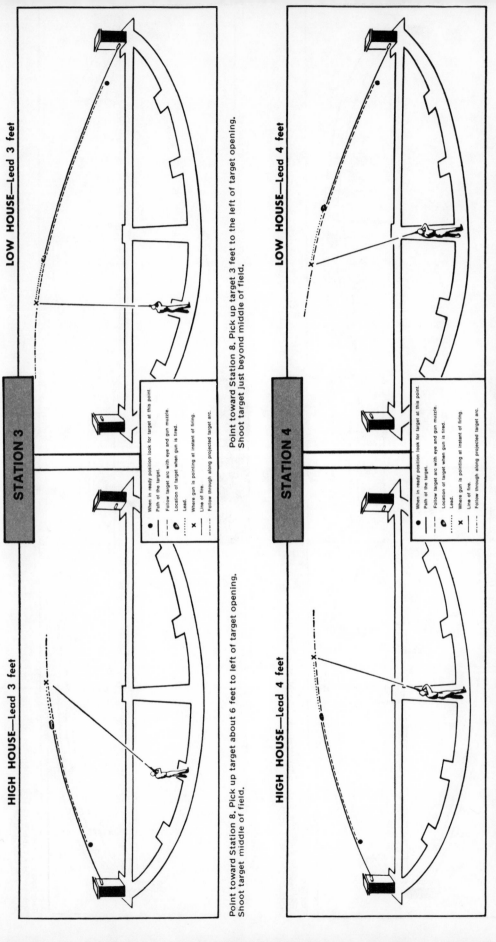

STATION 3

LOW HOUSE—Lead 3 feet

Point toward Station 8. Pick up target 3 feet to the left of target opening.
Shoot target just beyond middle of field.

HIGH HOUSE—Lead 3 feet

Point toward Station 8. Pick up target about 6 feet to left of target opening.
Shoot target just middle of field.

- ● When in ready position look for target at this point.
- --- Path of the target.
- ⬭ Follow target arc with eye and gun muzzle.
- ⋯⋯ Location of target when gun is fired. Lead.
- ✕ Where gun is pointing at instant of firing.
- —— Line of fire.
- —·—·— Follow through along projected target arc.

STATION 4

LOW HOUSE—Lead 4 feet

Point toward Station 8. Pick up target 3 feet to left of target opening.
Shoot target just to left of middle of field.

HIGH HOUSE—Lead 4 feet

Point toward Station 8. Pick up target 3 feet to the right of the target opening.
Shoot target just beyond the middle of the field.

- ● When in ready position look for target at this point.
- --- Path of the target.
- ⬭ Follow target arc with eye and gun muzzle.
- ⋯⋯ Location of target when gun is fired. Lead.
- ✕ Where gun is pointing at instant of firing.
- —— Line of fire.
- —·—·— Follow through along projected target arc.

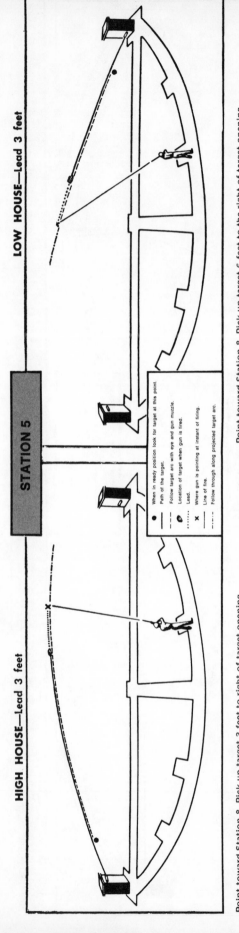

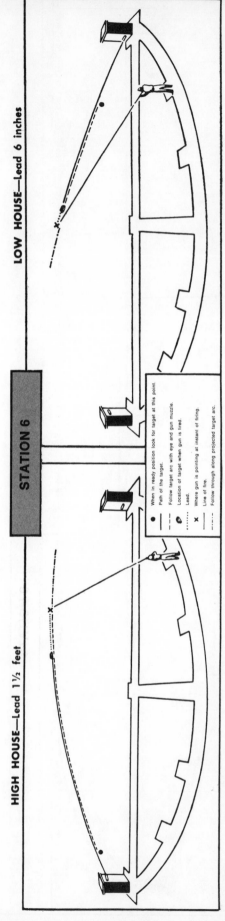

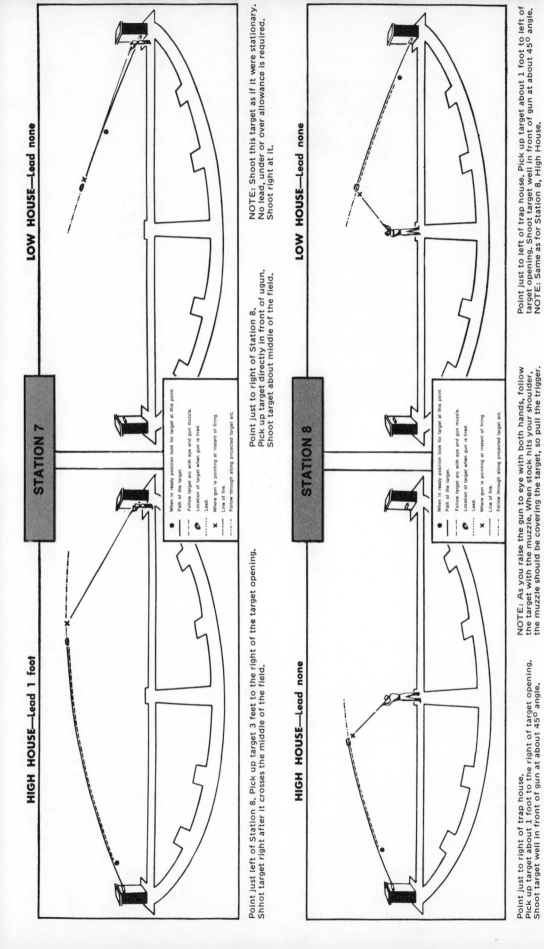

LOW HOUSE—Lead none

STATION 7

HIGH HOUSE—Lead 1 foot

Point just left of Station 8. Pick up target 3 feet to the right of the target opening. Shhot target right after it crosses the middle of the field.

Point just to right of Station 8. Pick up target directly in front of ugun. Shoot target about middle of the field.

NOTE: Shoot this target as if it were stationary. No lead, under or over allowance is required. Shoot right at it.

Legend:
- ● When in ready position look for target at this point.
- —— Path of the target.
- — — Follow target arc with eye and gun muzzle.
- ⋯⋯ Location of target when gun is fired.
- Lead.
- ✕ Where gun is pointing at instant of firing.
- —— Line of fire.
- —·—·— Follow through along projected target arc.

LOW HOUSE—Lead none

STATION 8

HIGH HOUSE—Lead none

Point just to right of trap house. Pick up target about 1 foot to the right of target opening. Shoot target well in front of gun at about 45° angle.

Point just to left of trap house. Pick up target about 1 foot to left of target opening. Shoot target well in front of gun at about 45° angle. NOTE: Same as for Station 8, High House.

NOTE.: As you raise the gun to eye with both hands, follow the target with the muzzle. When stock hits your shoulder, the muzzle should be covering the target, so pull the trigger.

Legend:
- ● When in ready position look for target at this point.
- —— Path of the target.
- — — Follow target arc with eye and gun muzzle.
- ⋯⋯ Location of target when gun is fired.
- Lead.
- ✕ Where gun is pointing at instant of firing.
- —— Line of fire.
- —·—·— Follow through along projected target arc.

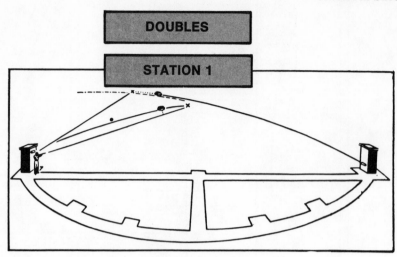

Point just to left of Station 8. Pick up target high in front of gun.
Shoot high house target just before it reaches middle of field, the low house just after
it passes middle of field.

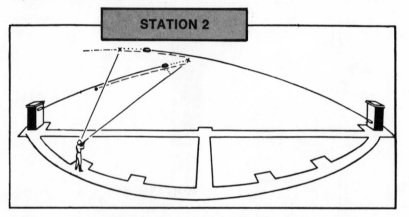

Point just left of Station 8. Pick up target about 12 feet to the right of the target
opening. Shoot high house target just before it reaches middle of field, the low
it passes middle of field.

between the two on a semi-circle with the first at the high house and the seventh at the low. An eighth post is located on a line halfway between the two houses. In a standard round of skeet, the shooter starts at Station 1 and shoots at a target from the high house. He then calls for a bird from the low house. He repeats this procedure at each station around the field. The targets always fly on the same path and varying angles are achieved by moving from one station to another. At Station 8, the one located between the two trap houses, the targets fly almost directly over the shooter's head and he must break them before they pass the center position of the field.

After touring the field once; shooting single targets as described above, the shooter returns to Station 1 for his doubles. Two targets are thrown simultaneously, one from the high house and one from the low. The shooter first tries to break the bird going away and then goes after the incomer. This procedure is repeated at Stations 2, 6, and

All about Skeet Shooting

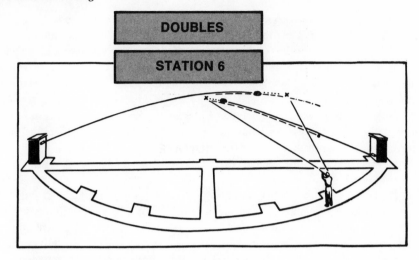

DOUBLES

STATION 6

Point just to the right of Station 8. Pick up target about 6 feet to the left of the low house target opening. Shoot the low house target about the middle of field, the high house after it passes middle of field.

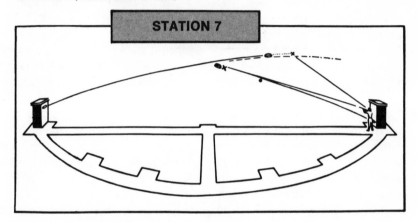

STATION 7

Point just to right of Station 8. Pick up target right in front of gun.
Shoot low house target just before it reaches middle of field, the high house just after it passes middle of field.

7. If the shooter has broken all of the targets thrown up until this point, he may take his 25th or "optional" shot, from any post that he desires. If he misses a bird earlier in the round, he repeats that target immediateily. As in trapshooting, one "round" consists of 25 targets.

The first skeet field was installed by Charles E. Davies and some friends at the Glen Rock Kennels near Reading, Massachusetts. For a number of years, the game was limited to this one field. In 1926, the late William H. Foster, editor of the *National Sportsmen* and *Hunting and Fishing* magazines, published stories about the layout in both publications. Foster, because of the work he did in promoting and refining the sport, is often called the "father of skeet." In addition to his promotional efforts, he also helped to christen the game, which had been nameless until that point. Over 10,000 entries were received in a contest he ran to find the best name. The winner, "skeet," which is an old Scandinavian word meaning "shoot," was submitted by Mrs. Gertrude Hulbert of Dayton, Montana.

Skeet caught on quickly after that. Within the next few years thousands of skeet clubs were organized, and skeet layouts were installed at existing gun clubs. The National Skeet Shooting Association was organized as the governing body for the sport. Today, registered tournaments, including the National Championships, are held under the auspices of the NSSA, which has its headquarters in Dallas, Texas, in much the same manner as trapshooting competition is handled by the Amateur Trapshooting Association.

Skeet today is one of our fastest growing participant sports. Competitions are held for four different gauges of shotguns, the 410, 28, 20 and 12, and the larger tournaments include events for all four shotguns.

Originally, the rules of the game required that shooters keep the gun butt below the waist when calling for the bird and there was a variation of up to three seconds between the time the shooter called "pull" and the time the target was thrown (the target could come out immediately or it might be delayed up to 3 seconds). In international competition, these rules still apply, but under the rules for competition in this country, the shotgun may now be mounted to the shoulder before calling for the bird, and targets are thrown instantaneously. In order to be sure that the puller knows which bird (high house or low house) the shooter is calling for, the call of "pull" is supposed to be used for the high house and "mark" for the low house.

Since target flight varies from straightaways at Stations 1 and 7, to shots that are at right angles, at Station 4, and incomers at Station 8, skeet fulfills its original intent of offering shooting situations more closely paralleling those found in hunting. The arguments among scattergunners who favor skeet over trap (or vice versa) about which

game is harder are legion. The trap fan claims that the unknown angles at which his targets fly provide more of an element of surprise—and thus requires more skill— while the skeet addict believes the wider variety of angles—even if known—are more challenging. There are a number of shooters who are proficient at and enjoy both games.

Any good upland shotgun can be used at skeet, provided the shooter is not out to win any major trophies. Because the average distance at which targets are broken is about 20 yards, the gun should have an open bore, which will deliver its most effective pattern at this distance.

Just as the trap shooter goes in for specially designed shotguns, so does the skeet fan. Stock dimensions of skeet guns are the same as those for field shooting—the straight stock of the trap gun would actually be a handicap. Barrels are usually 26 inches long, making for faster pointing at the relatively short ranges involved in skeet. Most shotgun manufacturers offer barrels with special "skeet" choke which gives a slightly tighter pattern than a plain open cylinder bore. Ventilated ribs on the barrels are preferred because they offer an even sighting plane.

Obviously, because of the requirements of the "doubles" phase of the game, skeet guns must be capable of firing two shots in rapid succession. Autoloaders, pumps, over-and-under doubles and side-by-side doubles are all popular. In recent years, the autoloaders, particularly the gas-operated models, have come into greater and greater popularity. Because these shotguns vent off some of the gas to operate the action, they are far lighter in recoil effect than fixed action models. In addition they are fast pointing, easy handling and capable of firing two shots just as fast as the shooter can pull the trigger.

The pumps and doubles still have their strong advocates, however, and many topflight shooters use them very effectively. In the last analysis, all four styles can do the job and it comes down to a matter of shooter preference.

The basic fundamentals of lead and form used in trapshooting also apply to skeet. Lead is the key to success. More targets are missed in both games because the shooter shoots behind them than for any other reason. As is the case with trapshooting, there are those who try to estimate the distance a shooter must shoot ahead of a target in order to hit it. Many of these people are eminent authorities on the sport and excellent shots.

Such considerations can be confusing to the beginner. The secret of success is the idea of "swing and follow through."

In hitting a golf shot, the player keeps his head down and his eyes on the ball. When he swings the club, he continues to look at the ball, and *after hitting it,* he continues his swing in a smooth follow through. If he tried to stop his swing at the moment of contact with the ball, he wouldn't have much luck. By the same token, the tennis player keeps his eyes on the ball—not the racket—and after hitting his shot, he continues to swing his racket in a smooth follow through. Without this follow through his shot would pop up in the air and go nowhere, except in the case of a volley at the net.

A shotgun shooter, whether he is on a skeet or trap field or after game, must follow the same principle. First of all, he looks at the target over his barrel, not at the barrel. In the second place, he must follow through in a smooth continuous motion, after touching off his shot.

It is obvious that the target must be led. The greater the angle, the greater the lead. By swinging the gun along the flight path of the target, pulling the trigger as the target is passed and following through, the shooter automatically calculates lead. He swings faster for the right or left angle than the straightaway, thus making his lead longer when it is necessary.

A relaxed stance is important. The feet should be about a foot apart with the weight on the forward one. They should be positioned to permit an easy, free swing along the flight path of the target. This will vary from station to station. If the shooter shoots from his right shoulder, the left foot should be advanced, and vice versa.

The best way to learn any sport is to go out and try it. Most gun clubs welcome beginners and will be glad to help them out. It's wise to start out with a good instructor so that the fundamentals can be learned properly at the start.

Four gauges of guns are used in skeet. The rules of the game specify that guns and ammunition in each gauge meet the following requirement:

410 (or sub-small bore) requires a gun of 410 gauge and shot of no more than ½-ounce no smaller than size 9

28 (or small bore) requires a gun of 28 gauge (or smaller) and restricts shot charge to ¾-ounce not smaller than size 9

20 gauge requires a gun of 20 gauge (or smaller) and restricts the shot size to ⅞-ounce not smaller than size 9

all-bore permits the use of a gun up to and including 12 gauge and restricts the shot charge to 1⅛ ounces not smaller than size 9

There are also requirements for maximum powder charges for each gauge. The ammunition companies all manufacture special shells designed for skeet shooting which meet these specifications.

In summary, the clay target sports, both trap and skeet, offer the field shooter an excellent means of sharpening his eye for hunting. More important, perhaps, both games are organized, recognized sports which offer good competition and plenty of fun for contestants.   T.M.C.

See also: HUNTING; RELOADING; SHOTGUNS.

How to Deal with Recoil

There are several steps you can take to reduce the shoulder-killing sting of a recoiling weapon—such as attaching a pad to the stock or wearing a well padded shooting jacket—but the principal means at your command is concentration

RECOIL IS THE REARWARD MOTION of the gun as it is being fired. The larger the caliber, the heftier the recoil, and gun makers build the kicking ones just a bit heavier. This helps to soak up that rearward motion, since the energy of the recoil has to overcome the inertia of the greater mass—spelled weight—of the heavy rifle or shotgun.

There are several ways to beat this thing called recoil. Most shooters, when handling a gun that kicks more than they are used to, don't really cradle the gun tightly into the shoulder. If there is one sure way to get your shoulder macerated and have it turn purple-blue-black, it is to hold the butt of the gun just a hair away from your shoulder. If you allow as much as ½-inch airspace between butt and shoulder, even a small caliber such as the .243 will eventually bruise your shoulder, and your scores.

If you feel that recoil is too much for you while sighting-in a hunting rifle, use a foam rubber pad between shoulder and butt. If recoil is still bothersome, either try a regular shooting jacket with a sewn-in pad, use more foam rubber, or buy yourself a 25 pound bag of No. 6 or 7½ shot. Place the bag between shoulder and butt, and you will hardly notice recoil.

Of course much depends on your shooting position. Shooting a gun with a fair amount of recoil from the prone position is asking for a beating. But there is no one who is totally immune to recoil. The trick is to learn how to lessen the kick.

Look at an experienced shooter sight-in his large caliber shotgun. He leans into the gun and then, when recoil strikes, he does not stiffen his torso, but lets recoil move him backward. This can be done while sitting at a shooting bench, kneeling, or shooting in the off-hand position, but in the prone position, everybody gets the same punishment. Here the brain and the eye take over.

Expert shooters concentrate every thought, and every bit of extra power they have or can muster goes into trigger control and the sight picture. The target shooter controls his breathing cadence carefully. Breathe in deeply, slowly exhale, repeat, then inhale and hold your breath while you align crosshairs and target. Try it—you'll suddenly find that you are so interested in the sight picture and your breath control that you hardly feel the kick of the shotgun —provided, of course, that you nestle the butt into your shoulder.

If that does not help, check the stock fit. If you suddenly discover that you are not very comfortable with the gun, have someone check the stock fit. Experienced shooters can adapt themselves to a poorly fitting stock, although it is not really the way to go about it. If you think that the stock may need some surgery, take the gun to a good gunsmith, or better yet, to a stockmaker if

▲ If you hunt big and dangerous game, the rifle you select must have the right amount of stopping power, and those calibers will also have a hefty recoil. It is therefore essential that the hunter becomes skilled in the use of a gun with heavy recoil as the .375 H&H shown here. Note how shooter bends with kick.

▲ The much more severe recoil of a .600 Nitro Express British double is shown in this picture. See how muzzle jump is much greater and the rearward motion is much more severe. Note also how the same shooter bends backward from waist thanks to recoil. The heavier the kick, the longer sight recovery time.

▲ Posed picture against white painted muzzle jump board shows how far a custom .338 Winchester Magnum with Pendleton muzzle brake brought gun upward. Such a muzzle brake helps considerably in reducing recoil and muzzle jump, but the gases forced out the side of the brake will certainly increase the blast.

▲ This is what the recoil of a .30-06 fired with the 180 grain factory load looks like in motion. Note how much higher the muzzle of the .30-06 rose than the muzzle of the .338 Winchester Magnum with the muzzle brake. If you are especially sensitive to recoil, installation of a muzzle brake might prove helpful.

there is one in your area. A good stockmaker can build up the comb or lower it, he can increase or shorten the length of pull, he can add pitch if need be, and he can install a thicker rubber recoil pad.

But if a weapon really doesn't fit you, then this sort of treatment may not help. If you are really attached to the shotgun and the caliber, you may be surprised to find that a not-too-fancy custom stock will not require a second mortgage. Of

course, it's almost impossible to fix costs of the wood—often called a stick by stockers —and on how much special work is needed. Naturally, the cost goes up when you get into fancy checkering, special carvings and custom features.

One often overlooked solution to the problem is to change to a self-loading weapon where the gas-operated mechanism soaks up much of the recoil. In shotguns, there are a number of very good gas-oper-

▲ *Here a shooter fires an off-hand 200 yards string with a .340 Weatherby.*

▼ *Custom muzzle brake or recoil compensator on custom .458 Winchester Magnum rifle.*

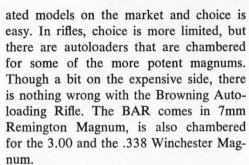

ated models on the market and choice is easy. In rifles, choice is more limited, but there are autoloaders that are chambered for some of the more potent magnums. Though a bit on the expensive side, there is nothing wrong with the Browning Autoloading Rifle. The BAR comes in 7mm Remington Magnum, is also chambered for the 3.00 and the .338 Winchester Magnum.

If you must shoot a rifle with hefty recoil and nothing else seems to help beat the flinches, a muzzle brake may be the answer. Some of these brakes are part and parcel of the muzzle of the barrel, others are threaded onto the muzzle and locked in place there. Basically, a muzzle brake consists of a series of carefully arranged slots or holes, slanted laterally, so that the powder gases are siphoned off before they leave the muzzle. High-speed photographic studies have shown that the gases exiting the muzzle, if bled off in this manner, no longer pack the recoil wallop they do when allowed to leave the muzzle in the usual manner.

Recoil compensators or muzzle brakes can be installed on any rifle barrel, and Weatherby's .460 Magnum rifle comes with a brake that soaks up quite a bit of the kick of this, the largest American cartridge.

However, before running to the nearest gun shop to order a brake, be forewarned about one thing—while recoil will be markedly reduced, muzzle blast will be more noticeable. What happens is that the gases are directed to the rear, and as they leave the confines of the barrel, the effect is somewhat like the sonic boom created by jets.

The last alternative is to say to yourself, time and again: "To heck with recoil, others can take it and so can I." It is really amazing how much you can accomplish this way. And when the word goes out that you can soak up recoil like a sponge, you'll be the hero of the local rifle range.   B.S.

See also: HUNTING; RELOADING; SHOTGUN.

Learn Shotgunning at Home

Practice with a BB gun. By the time you have fired off 1000 pellets, you will have confidence and shooting habits that can be transferred to shotgun shooting

YOU CAN LEARN TO BECOME a better shotgunner inexpensively by practicing with a BB gun. First get yourself a spring-type BB gun. Make sure it is a spring-plunger-type air gun, not a CO^2 gas gun.

A gas gun normally shoots in excess of 500 feet per second. This is too fast for the average eye to follow in flight. But a BB gun, such as a Model 99 Daisy lever action, has a velocity of about 325 feet per second. This is a speed that the average eye can follow in flight, and it is fast enough for accuracy while training.

When selecting a BB gun, also make sure that the distance from trigger to butt is about the same as your shotgun. You might have to add a very short wood spacer on the butt plate, but chances are you won't.

Next, you buy 1,000 BBs because you'll need them. Then, the final item is a half dozen 3-inch styrofoam balls, the kind used for decorating.

Now, remove the rear sight from your BB gun. This makes it more like a shotgun.

You are now ready for some practice. Try outdoors first. If your yard is large enough to provide a background of trees, shrubbery, or just open space, great; you have no need of a backstop.

But, if there's anything you don't want to hit within your BB gun's range, you'll need to fashion a backstop. This need not be larger than three feet square.

It can be an old rug suspended from a clothesline, or wire. Or, a corrugated box filled with folded newspapers will suffice. Anything which will stop, or absorb, the BB without making it ricochet.

A light background is best to see the BB in flight and a good distance to stand from the target is about 50 feet.

Your "bird" is going to be a 3-inch styrofoam ball suspended on a two-foot piece of string, hanging at rest in the center of the backstop.

Fill the magazine of your BB gun. Always keep the muzzle pointed skyward, except when you are on target ready to squeeze that trigger. Make certain no one is behind the backstop.

Now, with both feet comfortably apart, take a half step forward with the same foot as the hand which holds the forearm of the gun. In other words, if you hold the gun with your left hand, step forward with your left foot.

With your weight mostly on that forward foot, but enough on the rear foot to give you a sense of pivotal balance, slowly raise the BB gun to your shoulder and check how it cradles there—be sure it is solidly based.

If you are right-handed, keep your right elbow high as you grasp the pistol grip, butt against shoulder, and let your outer jaw come to rest alongside the gun stock.

Don't make the error of getting your head so low you are trying to sight down the barrel like on a rifle. The hollow of your cheek should be about even with the top of the stock. And it should come to rest there naturally and easily, without straining.

Now, with cheek resting on the stock, and your left hand cradling the foregrip as far forward as possible, slowly lower your right elbow and "lock" the gun butt against your right shoulder—at the same time firming your cheek against the stock.

shotgun patterning: see patterning, shotgun

This locks your shoulder and head to the stock, much the same as the interlocking grip on a golf club, and it is a highly important factor in accurate shotgunning.

Reason: this gives you a utilized movement of head and gun. In other words, when your head turns to follow game in flight, the gun barrel will be in position right between your eyes looking at the game.

This way you never have to worry about the gun being on the game and thus eliminate much of the problem of shooting behind or ahead of the game.

Practice this "double lock" hold a few dozen times, and remember this—you sight just over, not down the gun barrel, with both eyes open.

Get used to shooting with both eyes open. For a shotgunner this is not only faster but also safer. You quickly see whatever might be in, or coming into, your range before you pull the trigger.

When you've practiced enough to assume the proper shooting stance without having to think of each step, you're ready to squeeze off that first shot.

Envision yourself with an eyedropper between your thumb and forefinger. You're going to squeeze out one drop of water—no more!

This is the same kind of gentle squeezing action you should use on that trigger. You never jerk the trigger. To do so invites a miss because you can't jerk it the same each time—and you are not allowing the gun to do its own shooting.

With the eyedropper in mind, the gun "double locked" into position, and your balance comfortably accenting the forward foot—look with both eyes just over the barrel, centering on the styrofoam ball hanging 50-feet away.

Slowly, but steadily, squeeze the trigger and watch the BB go. Maybe at first your eye will fail to see it, but keep watching and it will loom sharp and clear.

Suppose you see it go high and to the left of the ball. Don't change anything until you've fired at least a dozen shots, or until you're fairly certain you're consistently shooting high and left.

To correct, you simply hold lower and right, until that styrofoam ball jumps with the impact of the BB.

You'll see why styrofoam is chosen for this practice. It is soft enough to absorb the BB, thus eliminating ricochet; and it's light enough to react when hit, giving you a responsive target.

Keep firing until you start to tire. Don't tax your endurance, even though your enjoyment still is high. When fatigue sets in, poor shooting and discouragement result.

As you put more hours behind the gun, you can shoot for an hour or so without tiring.

After a few hours practice, you not only should be hitting the ball four and five times in five shots, but also hitting the ball as it bounces and swings about.

This is excellent wing shooting practice because you're sighting on a moving target. And, when you're good enough, you can devise other moving targets like swinging cardboard discs, crisp crackers, or balloons.

For shooting indoors, follow the same procedure, plus adding an old blanket, or rug, for a backdrop. This eliminates the possibility of a stray shot doing any damage to furniture.

By the time you have shot 1,000 BBs using these fundamentals, you will: have creased a "memory track" which will enable you to shoot naturally without thinking about distracting details; shoot with confidence because you know you can hit a small target with a tiny BB—so you've got to hit a bigger target with that "bushel basket" pattern; be holding where you know you should hold, because you can see why and when you miss!

See also: HUNTING; SHOOTING.

The Basics of Shotgun Chokes

The choice of choke for your shotgun can make the difference between an empty game bag and a full one

BASICALLY, CHOICE OF CHOKE depends on the type of game you'll be hunting and the average distance at which most of your shots will be taken. The ideal for any range is to reach out with the largest possible pattern that still has enough pellet density to produce clean kills. A pattern that's too thin tends to produce crippled or lightly hit game.

One that's too tight promotes either misses or badly shot-up game. For close-up shots at about 20 to 25 yards, an improved cylinder will do nicely. This will open up your pattern quickly to the best size and density for effective results at such short range. Most quail, grouse and woodcock in heavy cover are taken with improved cylinder chokes.

For intermediate ranges between 25 and 35 yards, a modified or half choke is the ticket. This is the type of shooting that occurs most frequently when hunting pheasants in corn fields, rabbits in open cover or ducks over decoys.

Anytime you expect to be pegging pellets at game from 35 to 45 yards off, a full choke barrel is the correct choice. This will throw a tight pattern that opens up slowly and retains enough pellet density to remain effective past 40 yards.

These are the basic guides followed by most shotgunners, and if you follow them you won't ever be too far off. However, it isn't difficult to complicate the question of proper choke selection. For example, what about the situation in which you get a variety of shots at variable distances? Or when you're unlucky enough to miss the first shot and need a second, longer one? Or when you're trying for a double on feathered game and the second bird has powered a good way off before you can get around to him?

Probably the best answer to the variable range problem is to compromise by using a modified choke. Patterns from a modified choke barrel are understandably a bit tight for close game and somewhat thin for the long shots. But you can accommodate for this to some degree. Since a flushing bird or spooked game is more likely to be heading away from you than toward you, all you need do is ride your target out a way until it is at the proper range. This works

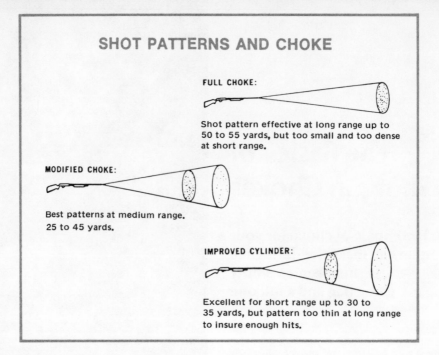

SHOT PATTERNS AND CHOKE

FULL CHOKE:

Shot pattern effective at long range up to 50 to 55 yards, but too small and too dense at short range.

MODIFIED CHOKE:

Best patterns at medium range. 25 to 45 yards.

IMPROVED CYLINDER:

Excellent for short range up to 30 to 35 yards, but pattern too thin at long range to insure enough hits.

reasonably well for short to medium-range shots. If the ranges tend to run from medium to long, you can accomplish the same thing by using a full choke barrel.

Another effective solution to the missed first shot or two-shot situation is the double barrel shotgun, either side-by-side or over-and-under. Excepting those designed for waterfowling, all double barrel shotguns have two chokes, relatively open in the first barrel and tighter in the second. If you'd normally be using an improved cylinder barrel, your double gun should combine that with a modified choke. Similarly, the modified and full choke combination would be correct for medium-range shooting because you'd often need the reach of the tight full choke by the time you got off the second shot.

There's also a way to handle increasing ranges when you're using a single barrel, repeating shotgun. You can do this by loading your gun with shells that have a progressively higher shot count. Here's an example of how this would work in a 12-gauge shotgun. You load the gun with three shells that contain 1-ounce, 1⅛-ounce and 1¼-ounce of shot respectively. Then, as the distance between you and the target

The amount of constriction in a shotgun's muzzle is referred to as the "choke." Different amounts of constriction give different sized patterns to a shot charge. For example, a full choke forces the shot charge closer together as it leaves the shotgun, delaying the tendency of the shot to spread. As a result, a full choke pattern is effective at greater distances. At close range, however, a full choke may be too small to insure being on target, or so dense that the game is ruined.

increases and the pattern gets larger, the higher shot count helps maintain pellet density.

For example, with No. 6 shot, a 1-ounce loading contains 350 pellets, 1⅛-ounce load about 394 pellets, and a 1¼-ounce load about 437 pellets. For the third shot, you could even use a standard-length magnum shell holding 1½-ounce of shot and 525 pellets.

Unfortunately, not all barrels marked with a given choke will perform the same, either in pattern density or in balanced distribution of pellets. There are variations from one manufacturer to another and even, on occasion, from barrel to barrel of the same maker. Generally, European-made barrels of a stated choke shoot tighter than American-made barrels of the same

The Basics of Shotgun Chokes 2413

designation. As a result, you can sometimes find barrels marked improved cylinder that will throw the equivalent of modified choke patterns, and barrels marked modified that come close to full choke performance.

Actually, there's only one way to determine exactly how your barrel shoots, and no shotgunner who wants good results in the field should skip this step. Take a few hours some day before the hunting season starts and carefully pattern your shotgun. What you discover can be an invaluable aid to better shooting. In the process you can also determine whether the barrel puts the shot pattern where it should and whether the stock fit enables you to point the gun correctly.

All you need is your shotgun, a couple of boxes of shells, some plain paper that measures at least 40 by 40 inches, and a back-up board that measures that size or larger. Set up the board two or three feet off the ground exactly 40 yards off. Then tack on the first sheet and in the center draw a black aiming spot about the size of a quarter. Fire at this spot by closing one eye and aiming directly down the barrel with the bead on the aiming spot. The resulting pattern should be spread evenly around the spot. If it isn't, you need a trip

to the gunsmith or a new barrel, because it isn't shooting where it's pointed.

On the next sheet, mount your gun as you would in the field and fire at the aiming spot with both eyes open. Again, the pattern should be centered around the spot. If it's high your stock is too straight for you. If it's low, the stock has too much drop.

Finally, if the pattern is hitting where it should, draw a circle with a 30-inch diameter around the aiming spot. Shoot from 25 yards away with an improved cylinder barrel, from 32 yards with a modified barrel, and from 40 yards with a full choke barrel. Move forward or back until you are getting about 70 to 75 percent of your pellets inside the circle. That distance, plus or minus a leeway of 5 to 7 yards, is the most effective shooting range.

If restricted to one choke for a variety of shooting, choose the modified choke. With light, 1-ounce loads it will suffice for close shooting. With heavy loads of 1¼-ounce or 1½-ounce it will give you fairly good results even on long shots. But since most shotguns today take interchangeable barrels, a modest investment in an extra barrel will set you up for virtually every type of hunting situation. T.F.

See also: HUNTING; PATTERNING, SHOTGUN; SHOT SHELLS; SHOOTING.

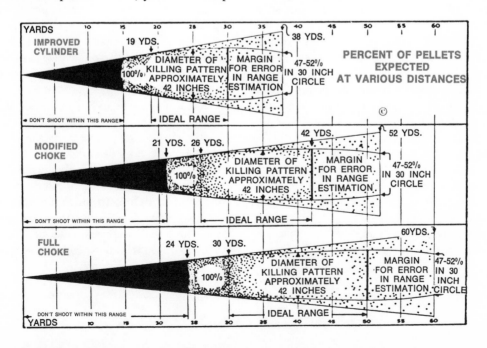

Selecting the Best Shot Size

Two factors govern your selection: the size of game you intend to kill and the range at which you plan to be shooting

THERE ARE REALLY TWO FACTORS you have to consider in selecting shot size. One is the type and size of the game you're hunting. The other is the range at which you expect to be shooting. Generally, the smaller the game, the smaller the shot size you should use. The greater the range, the larger the pellet size needed. These two generalizations may seem to conflict at times. For example, how do you figure which shot size is best for small birds at long distances? This doesn't usually create much of a problem. Most small birds such as quail, woodcock, and the like are hunted up close. While larger birds such as ducks, geese and wild turkey are generally shot at longer ranges.

Smaller pellets work better on small game for two reasons. Because these birds do provide shots at close range, open bored shotgun chokes that throw large, quick-opening patterns are used. Small shot sizes, which have more pellets per ounce, fill these patterns effectively, leaving no gaps to produce misses or cripples from lightly hit game. Larger pellets also tend to mangle small game making it unfit for the table. On those occasions where you might be shoot-

ing small game at fairly long range, you go up one shot size or so and use a tighter choke to keep the pattern from opening too quickly.

Larger shot sizes become necessary as range increases because the bigger pellets retain more energy at long range, while the small, No. 7½, 8 and 9 pellets are slowed down much more quickly by air resistance and run out of striking energy rapidly once they get 35 to 10 yards away.

Just for the sake of comparison, take a look at the difference in knock-down power at 50 yards of equal loads of No. 7½ and No. 2 shot, both fired from the same barrel. Assuming about a 70% pattern at that distance, there will be approximately 79 No. 2 pellets and about 306 No. 7½ pellets in-

shot size: see hunting

Selecting the Best Shot Size

side a 30-inch circle. The difference is great but the fewer number of 2's will actually have more total remaining energy at that distance than the far greater number of 7½'s. Furthermore, the 7½'s would be on the verge of being completely ineffective because they would barely penetrate the feathers of a large bird that far away.

As the range of your game decreases, though, the difference total energy delivered by small versus large shot also decreases. And you can gain in effectiveness from small shot by being able to use a more open choke, throwing a larger pattern still filled out with plenty of shot.

Opinions vary considerably on the best shot size for specific game. But here's a run-down of the general consensus among experienced hunters. In each case, the smaller shot size is for relatively close shooting with open chokes, and the larger shot for longer ranges with tighter chokes. For quail, woodcock and rail birds, use 7½'s to 9's. For dove, band-tailed pigeons, ruffed grouse and Hungarian partridge, use 6's to 8's. For Western grouse, pheasant, rabbits and squirrels, use 5's to 6's. Ducks, use 5's to 7½'s. And for turkeys, geese and foxes, use 2's to 4's.

Trying to pick a single shot size that's best for a variety of game creates the same result as trying to select a single rifle caliber for all big game. You're always going to be overgunned or undergunned for some species.

However, if you can only take along one shot loading with no previous knowledge of what game you will be seeing, it should be No. 6 shot. No. 6's are just right for medium-size game, have enough pellets to provide hits on small birds, and will even down geese if you limit your shooting range. Obviously 6's are the first choice of the greatest number of hunters because the ammunition manufacturers sell more shells in this size than any other.

It is also an excellent idea to pattern your

shotgun to see how it performs with different shot sizes. Some barrels apparently produce more evenly distributed patterns with one shot size than another. For instance, you may find a barrel producing patterns with gaps in them from one size shot, while it will produce a nicely-balanced spread of pellets from one size larger or smaller. This may be why some shotgunners argue so vehemently in favor of one particular shot size over another. It may well be that their tube just performs better with what has become their pet pellet size.

However, if you're consistently missing more birds than you think you should, the problem may be just a lack of sufficient practice. Put in some time during the off season on trap and skeet clay targets so you can learn better what leads you need for the various angles they produce. You'll find your field shooting will sharpen up in direct relation to the amount of practice you take. T.F.

See also: HUNTING; PATTERNING, SHOTGUN; RELOADING; SHOOTING; SHOTGUN.

▼ *It is a good idea to pattern your shotgun to see how it performs with different shot sizes.*

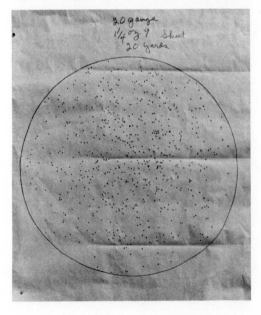

Portable Shower for Your Camper or Trailer

This collapsible unit stows in a small place and provides a refreshing shower at the end of a day outdoors with water warmed by the sun

WITH THIS INEXPENSIVE homemade portable shower one can have refreshing evening baths when camping, using water warmed by midday sun.

The shower is erected quickly and easily, as all parts slip or snap together, except the hose and head assembly which has a garden hose connection to the supply tank. The tank shown is a thin steel drum holding seven gallons of water, enough for three baths. It is placed on top of the camper trailer by using the back of a pickup truck, a car, or a step ladder to stand on. If lifting is done by one person, it is easier if the container is not completely full of water. There are various containers available which should make suitable supply tanks. The shape is not too important, but metal is more effective than plastic in conducting heat from the sun or other sources to warm the water. The water can become surprisingly warm exposed to midday sun, although air temperatures are well under eighty degrees. Plastic containers should

▲ This portable shower affords enough water for three baths. Curtain is made of blue denim with snaps at the front.

Portable Shower for Your Camper or Trailer 2417

◄*Framework of shower goes together readily.*

▼ *Tank shape is unimportant, but its material —metal or plastic—will affect sun's ability to warm water. A couple of wood strips keep tank from rolling.*

▼ *Component parts of the shower are easily stored in your trailer and are lightweight. Frame is 1/2-inch conduit. Various containers would do for tank.*

2418   *Portable Shower for Your Camper or Trailer*

work well, providing the water is first heated on a stove or over a campfire and then put into the tank. In the cool of the evening, water will stay warm longer in a plastic tank than in a metal one, though, of course, the inconvenience of heating water is added.

The frame is made of ½-inch electrical conduit which is strong and light in weight. The lower ends of the vertical pieces fit snugly into ¾-inch diameter holes drilled into the corners of the wooden base; the upper ends have metal pins which insert through holes in the corners of the top frame. The curtain is made of blue denim snapped together at the entrance and hung from the shower curtain rings by grommets. The shower head assembly consists of a sprinkler, an "on-off" valve, and an 18-inch length of ½-inch garden hose, attached to the tank with an externally threading fitting. The hardware is standard and can be purchased at most any hardware store.

During assembly the wooden base should be thoroughly dry because of the close fit between the vertical pieces and the holes in the base.   H.R.G.

See also: CAMPERS; CAMPING; CAMPING EQUIPMENT; TRAILER, TENT.

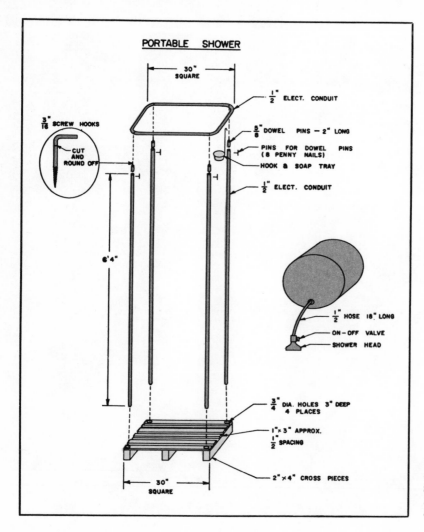

◄ *Construction details of the portable shower. Hardware is available anywhere.*

Install a Break-resistant Acrylic Shower Door

This simple job could spare someone in your family serious injury

A CRYLIC GLAZING MATERIAL is safer to use than glass in the doors of shower compartments, although it can be more expensive. Acrylic sheeting breaks less easily than glass and when it does shatter, it cracks into large pieces with fairly dull edges. There are no razor-sharp jagged shards and splinters to cause serious injury.

To replace the glass in the shower door with acrylic sheet, remove the door and lay it flat on a worktable. If the glass has been broken, use extreme care and pull out any loose pieces first.

With the door lying flat, remove the screws at all four corners of the frame. Using a screw driver and a hammer, gently tap off the top and bottom pieces and disassemble the entire frame.

Remove any glass. Pull the rubber gasket from the frame and clean it. Measure the size of the opening that the acrylic is to fit. Do this accurately. Then, deduct $\frac{1}{32}$ of an inch for each foot of length and each foot of width. The deduction for each dimen-

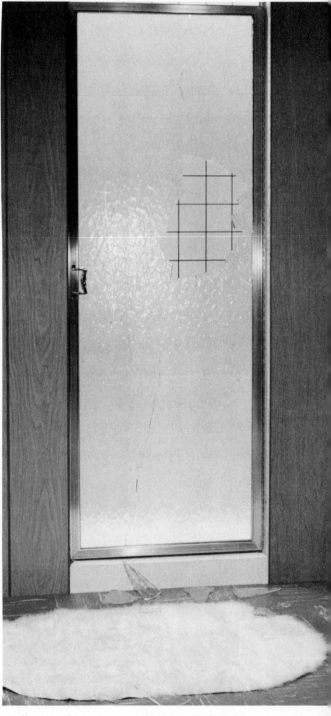

▲ If your glass shower compartment door is broken, you can replace it easily with one of break-resistant acrylic sheeting.

2420

⬆ After removing any loose glass that might fall on you while you work, remove the door.

⬆ Lay the door flat on a worktable and pull out any additional loose glass.

⬇ Tap the top and bottom pieces gently to remove them from the frame.

⬆ To disassemble the door, remove the screws at each corner.

Install a Break-resistant Acrylic Shower Door

▲ *Fit the rubber gasket around the acrylic sheet.*

▼ *Press the door frame pieces gently over the gasket on all four sides, replace the screws at the corners and rehang the door.*

Leave the masking paper on each side while you cut and while you sand the edges. The edges do not require a transparent finish, but should be sanded smooth with medium-grit abrasive paper. This will increase the acrylic's resistance to breakage.

When the sheet is cut and the edges are smooth, remove the masking paper from each side and fit the rubber gasket all around it. Press the door frame pieces gently over the gasket on all four sides. Replace the door screws at the corners and rehang the door. The job is done.

See also: ALUMINUM; ENCLOSURE, BATHROOM; GLASS; STORM DOORS AND WINDOWS; WINDOWS.

▼ *The completed shower door.*

sion will give the acrylic sheet room for thermal expansion.

Order ⅜-inch-thick acrylic for your door. You can use smooth surfaced sheet or one with a pattern embossed on one or both sides. Clear and several colors are available. The easiest way to cut the acrylic is to order it to size and let your supplier do the work.

If you cut it yourself, use a circular saw with a fine-tooth plywood or veneer blade.

How to Build Your Own Shutters

Shutters provide a decorative way to control light and ventilation at windows, but they have other uses too, such as covering bookcases or in room dividers, or a pass-through between kitchen and dining area

⊼ Interior shutters add functional decoration to modern or traditional rooms. Dividing shutters into two panels provides ultimate in light and ventilation control.

WINDOWS ARE NOT THE ONLY places for shutters. Shuttered bookcases can add a note of charm. Shutters can also cover a basement window or serve as a closet or rumpus room door.

You can build and fit your own shutters. To fit a window with shutters—either all the way to the top or only part way up from the bottom, first measure width of window between faces of casing. Height runs from sill to face of upper casing and may be divided at any point, although the dividing line between upper and lower shutters usually looks best when lined up with meeting rails of a double-hung window.

Divide the width of the opening into four equal parts. From the height measurement, figure how many vanes you'll need. Use sugar pine for shutters. Saw rails and stiles (two of each are needed for each panel) from 1 x 6-inch stock (¾ x 5⅝-inch) and the vanes from 1⅛-inch thick stock. To make a bead about ³⁄₁₆-inch from outer edge of stiles, nick the front face with

the table saw set at 45°, then sand corners round.

Cut the 1⅛-inch vane stock to lengths equal to the width of the stiles less ¹⁄₃₂-inch for clearance as shown in the drawing. For uniformity, set a gage block on your table saw. Use a hollow-ground planer-type saw blade to minimize sanding. Next, locate and mark the centerline down each end of each section for later location of nail pivots. Rip the vanes ³⁄₁₆-inch thick.

Clamp the vane ends in a vise, keeping the tops flush with the vise top to prevent splitting, then drive 3-penny finishing nails into the vane ends. Clip off the nail heads, leaves about ⅜-inch projecting for pivots.

After marking a centerline along the inside face of the stiles, clamp them together and mark pivot points across stiles. Distance between bottom rail and first pivot

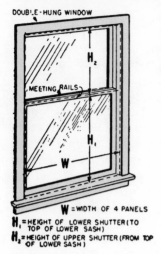

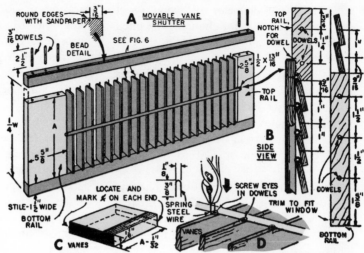

and between top pivot and top rail should be $\frac{9}{16}$-inch. When pivots are spaced 1-inch, vanes overlap $\frac{1}{16}$-inch in closed position. Using a sharp (60° angle) center punch, mark pivot hole centers. Clamp a guide board or fence to the drill press table and drill $\frac{1}{16}$-inch holes $\frac{1}{2}$-inch deep at the marked centers.

Now, you're ready to assemble the parts. Dowel fasten the rails to one stile, forming a U-shaped frame. Insert vanes, then fit second stile over vane pivots. Align stiles to rails with an adjustable wood clamp. Drill holes through stiles and $\frac{1}{2}$-inch deep and $1\frac{1}{2}$ inches apart into rails and glue $\frac{3}{16}$-inch diameter dowels in place. Trim dowels flush with edge and plane smooth.

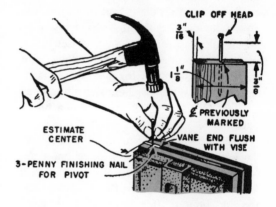

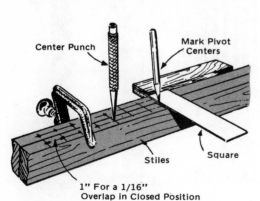

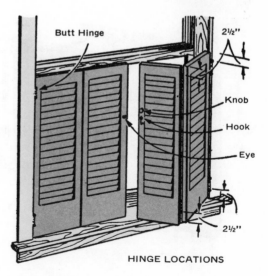

HINGE LOCATIONS

Use a ⅜-inch diameter soft wood dowel with chamfered ends for changing the pitch of the vanes. On a dowel as long as the distance between the bottom rail and the top rail, mark off spacing for the screw eyes and drill pilot holes. Use small screw eyes, about $\frac{3}{32}$ to ⅛-inch inside diameter. Try a picture-framing studio for these if your hardware store doesn't have them. Use a small center punch or nail to help turn screw eyes.

Next, staple the adjuster dowel into the vane edges. Cut #26 or 28 gage steel spring wire, available at hardware stores, into ¾ to ⅞-inch lengths and form them into staples. Ready-made staples that small are not generally available. Grasp each staple in turn in a pliers and press into the vane with one leg through the screw eye. When all vanes are attached, chisel out a pocket in the upper rail for the dowel end so vanes nest together for maximum shade.

Sand the shutters, then spray them as desired. Or use a small brush plus a bit of patience.

Use butt hinges to mount the shutters. To join panels of shutters along one side, lay the two shutters face down and screw 2 x 2-inch butt hinges to the back near the top and bottom. If you use a three-panel section, or more, alternate the hinges on back and front so panels fold together accordion fashion.

Attach each group of panels to window casing by mortising hinges into edge of shutter stile and window frame. Set hinges out far enough so shutters fold back against trim molding around window, parallel with the face trim of window or door. Where shutter panels meet, attach knobs for swinging them open and a hook and eye across the opening to keep panels in a closed position.

Making vanes adjustable isn't necessary for some applications, such as for closet doors or folding screens. For fixed-vane applications, measure shutters in the same way as for movable vane shutters. Vanes, this time the width of the stiles plus ⅜-inch, fit into slanting slots cut in the inside faces of stiles instead of using pivots. Because vanes are cut off at a 45° angle, they can be cut from the same stock as the shutter frames. Fit a ⅛ x ⅜-inch bead molding along inner sides of stiles to cover notches. Or, frame the entire shuttered opening in each panel with the molding. Hinge panels together and attach in window openings as shown.   M. E. D., D. M. S.

See also: ROOM DIVIDERS; WOODWORKING.

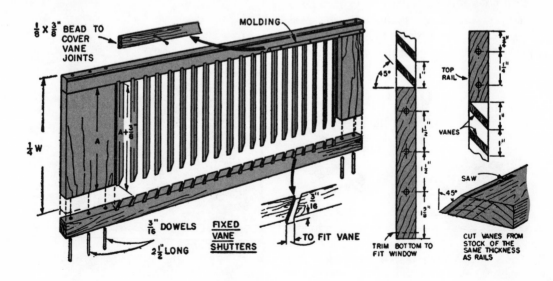

⅛ X ⅜" BEAD TO COVER VANE JOINTS

MOLDING

¼ W

A

A+⅜"

3/16" DOWELS

2½" LONG

FIXED VANE SHUTTERS

TO FIT VANE

45°

TOP RAIL

VANES

SAW

45°

TRIM BOTTOM TO FIT WINDOW

CUT VANES FROM STOCK OF THE SAME THICKNESS AS RAILS

↑ Knotty grades of board siding give a rustic appearance to a home at a price much lower than for clear grades.

How to Select Siding for Your Home

**Use this guide to thread your way through
the variety of sidings available to
find the one that suits your house
and your pocketbook**

Exterior siding is the "suit of clothes" that your home will wear for many years to come. That suit is subject to public scrutiny day in and day out, hence you should pick siding that will enhance the basic architectural character of your home. But appearance isn't everything, any more than it is with the clothes you wear yourself. Your home, too, deserves an outer wrap that is also warm and durable. And you

want these desirable features—good appearance, weather resistance and durability—at reasonable cost. The only way you can be sure of outfitting your new home properly is to learn as much as possible about the strengths and weaknesses of different types of siding materials.

This is not particularly easy: there are almost too many types and styles to consider. You can't just settle on wood board siding, for example, because there are many different types of board siding. If you favor hardboard panels, you must decide which of the many available colors and textures would be most appropriate.

▲ *Softwood plywood sidings can be ordered smooth or textured and may be stained or painted. Surface textures include rough sawn, brushed or smooth. Usually available in Douglas fir, southern pine, redwood and knotty cedar. Face patterns include channel groove, reverse board-and-batten and ungrooved.*

If you haven't yet narrowed the possibilities to one or two general siding types, you will have to start by eliminating most of the following available siding materials: shingles and shakes, wood board siding, plywood panels, hardboard panels, aluminum siding with baked-on enamel finish, asbestos-cement siding, asphalt shingles, roll siding, stone, stucco, brick, nail-on brick, molded brick and stone, prefinished fiberboard and vinyl (plastic) siding.

The problem can be simplified somewhat by categorically eliminating some of these. Roll siding, made to look like brick or stone, is not sufficiently durable; and worse, it could make your home look like an oversize chicken coop. Asphalt shingles are fine for the roof, but on walls they are easily damaged and their mineral coatings tend to fall off. Some home-building experts also reject stucco (prone to form hairline cracks), nail-on brick (develop cracks too easily), molded brick or stone (joints may open), and fiberboard (easily damaged). However, some of these materials have legitimate uses that will be mentioned later.

Board siding. If you think that "clapboard" siding is still popular, you couldn't be more wrong. Old-fashioned clapboard was cut in a particular way from timber; it's not done that way any more, even though some siding still looks much like clapboard.

Board siding is made from a variety of woods including Douglas fir, spruce, hemlock, redwood, cedar, cypress and both white and yellow pine. The rarer and/or more durable woods command the higher prices. But price is materially affected by other factors as well, notably the amount of millwork required to make each style of board siding.

The least expensive is common bevel siding. These are merely boards tapered so that one edge is thinner than the opposing edge. The thin edges are lapped under the thick edges of successively higher boards. Bevel siding is more likely to warp than those that have locking joints. Tongue and groove drop siding, including the style called "novelty" siding, provides a tight, weatherproof joint that also eliminates board warping. Rabbeted joints are an improvement over simple lap joints (bevel siding), but they do not lock together as securely as do tongue and groove joints.

Note that some types of siding provide slightly angled board surfaces whereas others provide basically flat surfaces broken up by longitudinal grooves of one shape or other. The overall textural or pattern effect that each style creates derives partly from the board shape, and partly from the

▼ *Bevel siding is the simplest and least expensive; the tapered boards are simply lapped when laying. Tongue & groove novelty offers greater structural strength and sealing, and a basically flat rather than beveled wall surface. T & G drop and rabbeted drop look much like common bevel with tighter interlocking joints.*

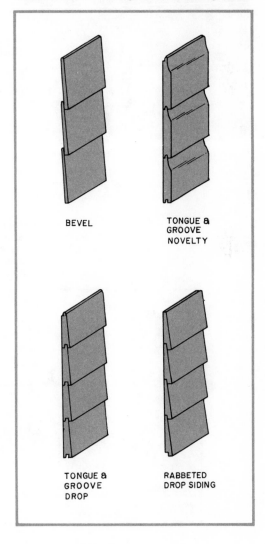

BEVEL

TONGUE & GROOVE NOVELTY

TONGUE & GROOVE DROP

RABBETED DROP SIDING

⋀ *Large sheets of wood siding can cover a lot of square footage in one application, greatly reducing labor costs.*

⋁ *Shiplap and channel rustic have rabbeted joints and are similar except one has a curved groove while other is angular. Double V-rustic is identical with V-rustic except that each board has an extra V groove that simulates a joint.*

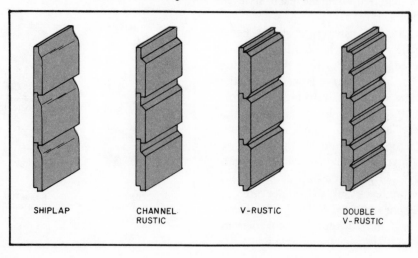

SHIPLAP　　CHANNEL RUSTIC　　V-RUSTIC　　DOUBLE V-RUSTIC

shadow patterns that the grooves or over-hangs produce. Thus two otherwise identi-cal homes can look significantly different if different types of board siding are utilized.

Shakes and shingles. Wood shingles and shakes are basically the same except that shakes have scored faces and they are as much as three feet long so that a larger area of each piece can be exposed to weathering. Shingles and shakes continue to be popular

▼ *Pre-painted lap siding can reduce your over-all paint costs. You can combine it with matched soffits and pre-finished windows for exterior that is virtually finished.*

because they are moderate in price, and because they are easy to maintain in good condition. There are purists who feel that shingles should be allowed to age naturally, and should not be painted. But many main-tain that shinges that are stained or painted periodically look better, and are less likely to warp or crack or curl.

If you are having a hard time deciding between shingles and wood board siding, look about your neighborhood and see which material is more prone to produce paint blistering and peeling. Most likely, you will find more peeling on board siding than on shingles. This is not to discourage

➤ *Asbestos shingles may be cut, sawn and worked like wood. With factory-applied colors permanently sealed within, the need for frequent repainting and maintenance is eliminated. One of the biggest benefits is that asbestos shingles will not burn. Available in many popular colors.*

▼ *Best brick facing for frame house is built of standard size bricks. Main support is provided by solid concrete base while anchor irons are used only to keep wall from toppling over, thus shifting of house in settling is not likely to develop cracks.*

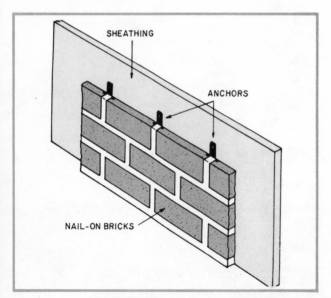

SHEATHING

ANCHORS

NAIL-ON BRICKS

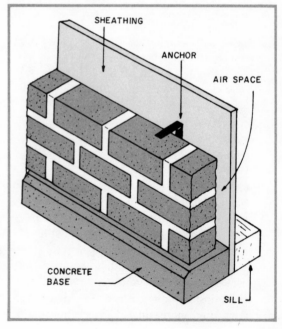

SHEATHING

ANCHOR

AIR SPACE

CONCRETE BASE

SILL

▲ *Thin nail-on brick or simulated stone are relatively inexpensive. Thin bricks are anchored to sheathing with special anchor clips and spaces between bricks are filled with cement. If house frame shifts in settling, this type wall may develop cracks.*

How to Select Siding for Your Home

you from using board siding if it looks best on your home; just be prepared to work a little harder to keep it looking good.

Plywood. The unusual physical strength of plywood makes it a top contender as a siding material in areas where hurricanes or earthquakes can be expected. You can use unfinished plywood and finish it yourself, or save a lot of time and labor by using factory prefinished plywood that is treated with polyvinyl-chloride coating materials. The prefinished plywoods are "guaranteed" to never require painting. But "never" implies a very long time indeed, so find out whether the guarantee relates to appearance as well as to resistance to weathering. Textured plywoods can be very attractive, but bear in mind that rough textured materials are harder to clean than are smooth.

Hardboard. Prefinished hardboard is made from wood fibers that are permanently bonded, by application of heat and pressure, to form a tough "engineered" wood that is highly resistant to denting, cracking, warping and weathering. However, hardboard is not as strong as plywood. This relatively new siding material is approved by FHA and general building codes. Hardboard siding is available in many forms, including lap siding and large panels embossed with grooves, shingle-like patterns, and realistic wood textures. They come in many attractive colors. Top-quality hardboards carry double guarantees: 10 to 15 years warranty against color deterioration, and 25 years against "hail damage." If you live in termite country, or if other insects that destroy wood are abundant, hardboard may be a good choice because of its resistance to insect damage and rot.

Metal and plastic. Prefinished aluminum siding is moderately expensive—more costly than plywood and competitively priced with better grades of board siding when installation costs are added. It is being used increasingly on new housing as

well as for reconditioning older homes. Aluminum is durable and easy to keep clean, but it can be dented. Some manufacturers of aluminum siding guarantee the baked-on enamel for twenty years or more.

▼ *Comparison of the relative costs of different siding materials should include installation labor costs since these can significantly alter the relative total costs. Actual prices are not indicated because local materials and labor costs may differ markedly from these national averages. Use this chart only as a general guide. (¹C grade or better. ²Rustic or shiplap. ³Paint grade.) These prices don't include accessories.*

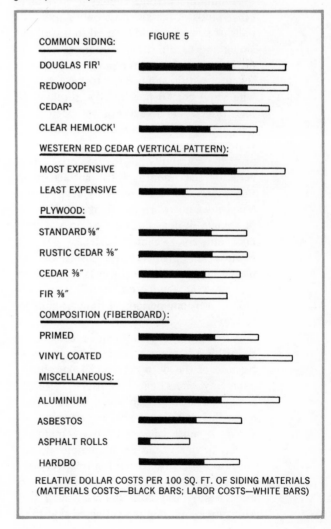

COMMON SIDING: FIGURE 5

DOUGLAS FIR¹
REDWOOD²
CEDAR³
CLEAR HEMLOCK¹

WESTERN RED CEDAR (VERTICAL PATTERN):
MOST EXPENSIVE
LEAST EXPENSIVE

PLYWOOD:
STANDARD ⅜"
RUSTIC CEDAR ⅜"
CEDAR ⅜"
FIR ⅜"

COMPOSITION (FIBERBOARD):
PRIMED
VINYL COATED

MISCELLANEOUS:
ALUMINUM
ASBESTOS
ASPHALT ROLLS
HARDBO

RELATIVE DOLLAR COSTS PER 100 SQ. FT. OF SIDING MATERIALS
(MATERIALS COSTS—BLACK BARS; LABOR COSTS—WHITE BARS)

Aluminum offers no insulating benefits, as do other kinds of siding such as wood or hardboard; hence extra insulation is generally used, often in the form of plastic foam placed directly under the siding.

Aluminum is impermeable to water vapor, and the house will not be able to "breathe" as it should unless venting systems are provided. Each space behind the siding can be ventilated by means of small, weatherprotected horizontal openings; or if the siding is fastened to furring strips vent openings can be used at the top and bottom of each space between furrings.

Aluminum corrodes rapidly if it contacts other kinds of metals, thus only aluminum nails or screws should be used to install the siding and to add other mountings such as metal hangers for drain pipes.

Vinyl plastic siding (not to be confused with vinyl coated fiberboard) is relatively high priced and it has not yet been used long enough to have stood the test of time. However, there's no reason to doubt the probable durability of the material. And certainly the smooth plastic surface must rate as one of the easiest to keep clean. Vinyl does not warp as might wood siding or shingle, it does not dent as does aluminum, and colors cannot blister or peel off because the pigments are inside of the plastic, not on the surface as a separate coating. Whether the colors will withstand fading over long periods of time remains to be seen.

Although vinyl siding can be broken by sharp blows, minor scratches do not show because of the deep coloring. Like aluminum, vinyl offers negligible insulating value, hence extra insulation may be required. Since this material is also impermeable to vapor, it must be ventilated by methods similar to those used for aluminum siding.

Masonry facings. Brick is a relatively expensive siding material, and stone is even more costly. But both materials will last with minimum attention provided that they

are installed properly. If the work is done by an incompetent workman, you may have problems with cracking and efflorescence (the development of unsightly white powder accumulations and stains on and around the cement). Stone does not show dirt easily, but cleaning is quite difficult when it is needed because of the rough texture. Brick is likewise harder to clean than are smooth siding materials.

Thin nail-on bricks are fastened directly to the house sheathing using special metal holders. This is the cheapest way to obtain a brick-faced house. But if the house frame shifts because of settling or for other reasons, the brickwork is bound to develop cracks. The problem may not be serious if the brick is applied to an old house that has settled about as much as it can or will.

Cracking because of house settling is not as likely to occur if standard brick facing is used. Instead of being fastened to the house sheathing, brick by brick as in the case of nail-on brick, the larger bricks are built onto a solid concrete base. A narrow air space is left between the bricks and the sheathing. The metal anchors are used only to keep the wall from toppling over. If the house frame moves a bit, these anchors can flex and take up strain that would otherwise damage the brickwork.

Stucco has a tendency to develop hairline cracks, and chipping can occur if the house moves. But if your heart is set on a Spanish or Mediterranean style home, you will have to live with this possible drawback because most other siding materials would be inappropriate for such architectural styles. Just make certain that your stucco home is sturdily built on a solid base—especially if the home is more than one story high.

Asbestos-cement siding is not "masonry" in the usual sense; however it has a remote kinship to such materials because it is of mineral composition. Asbestos-cement siding is available as sheets, shingles or "clap-

▲ *Two different sidings can be used on a home: aluminum and brick and vinyl and brick. Aluminum is moderately expensive but will require extra insulation in colder climates. Vinyl siding, both vertical and horizontal are shown here, never needs painting.* ◄

boards." It should be considered when moderate cost and long-term durability are important factors. Extremely good fire resistance is another plus. Asbestos-cement is virtually indestructible (except for cracking if struck hard) even if it is never painted. However, it accepts paint readily, or you can buy types that have factory-applied plastic finishes.

Cost comparisons. Installation labor costs are not identical for all kinds of siding; thus it is important to include labor costs when comparing the costs of different siding materials.

The comparative price chart shown here does not indicate actual dollar values because the comparisons reflect nationwide averages for many sidings that fall into each category. Local prices may differ significantly from these average prices, as may installation costs. For example, Douglas fir siding is available in various grades and widths ranging from four inches to 12 inches. Prices vary from $36 to $44 per square (100 square feet) for grade C or better siding. Labor costs also vary, mainly because of board width differences since it is more time-consuming to cover a given wall area using narrow boards than if wide boards are used. It might cost $23 to install a square of three inch wide siding, but only $17.25 using 10 inch or 12 inch siding.

Bearing in mind that the chart represents averages of such price ranges, it may be helpful to note that the combined material and labor costs for Douglas fir siding totaled about $56 per square at the time the figures were compiled. By the time you read this, the price may be higher because of inflationary pressures.

Maintenance. There's no such thing as a completely maintenance-free siding material since the most durable wall material at least needs an occasional cleaning. Well-constructed brick and stone facings, asbestos-cement siding (unpainted), alumi-num siding with baked-on finish and vinyl siding are among the most maintenance-free materials now available. But remember that even these materials may require some work to keep them in good shape. Brick and stone facings may develop cracks requiring filling, and efflorescence may have to be removed periodically. Asbestos-cement shingles, if broken, must be replaced promptly. Vinyl and aluminum sidings can be severely damaged by falling trees, land slides, out-of-control vehicles and the like. If such damage is sustained 10 years after installation of the siding, can you be certain that replacement siding of the same color will still be available, or that the "green" vinyl or aluminum siding you buy to patch a damaged area will match the weathered "green" then on your house?

Undoubtedly the most common maintenance problem concerns periodic repainting of wood siding (board, shingle or plywood). You must count on repainting light-colored woods every four years, darker woods every five or six years. It's a mistake, incidentally, to paint too often. The new paint will not bond properly to old paint unless the existing paint has had time to age properly. Stained shingles also need re-staining about every five or six years. Mildew can attack wood siding in shaded, damp locations. It should be removed before repainting by scrubbing down with detergent to which chlorine bleach has been added.•

To anticipate other possible maintenance problems consult other reference works for additional information about siding materials. Learn all you can about siding by talking with your building contractor or lumber company representative. Don't leave all the decisions to others. After all, the "suit of clothes" you put on your new home will reflect your taste and not that of outsiders involved in the construction. J.H.

See also: HOME IMPROVEMENT; HOME OWNERSHIP; PAINTING, HOUSE; STUCCO.

Stopping Leaks in Wood Siding

Moisture penetrating your house's siding can lead to decay and plaster damage. The place to stop it is at the walls

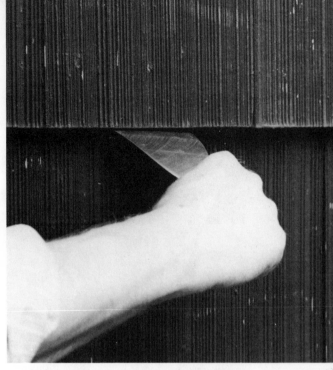

PLITS IN WOOD SIDING, loose knots, leaks in flashing, all invite moisture to enter wood walls and start costly decay in your home. Fungi, which feed on damp wood, hasten the progress. And, if water can continue to enter, you may also get water-stained and weakened plaster walls and ceilings in the interior.

The best attack on the moisture problem is to give the house a complete inspection. Be sure gutters and drains are clear, and check around edges of roof and near chimneys and windows for leaks in flashing, or other materials. Then check the siding for looseness, splits or breaks.

Nail down any loose siding you find. If the siding is badly split or decayed, replace it. Bore a hole near a stud, so you can cut along the stud with a compass saw or an electric saber saw. Split out the damaged wood and use an old chisel or tire iron to pry up the lower edge of the siding board above. If there is danger of splitting this next board, slide a hacksaw blade between the boards and saw through the nails. Work the heads of the nails out of the board above. Use a nail set to drive the nail stubs in, and you can remove the board.

The new siding board should be face-primed and back-primed first. Where there is no sheathing, nail 1 x 3-inch strips to the sides of the 2 x 4 studs to catch the ends

▲ *Check your wood siding for leaks and scrape away loose paint. Small splits and knots can be patched. Large cracks may require replacing section of siding.*

of the new piece. Over sheathing, use a circular saw (set to shallow depth), or a chisel, to cut the edge of the board at the joint.

If a board is sound and free of decay, but has a loose knot, or a small split, you can make a neat patch repair. Clean the area removing scaling paint and dirt with a wire brush. For a knothole, use a disc larger than the resinous rim of the knot; for a

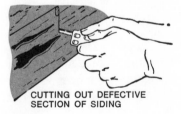

CUTTING OUT DEFECTIVE SECTION OF SIDING

TRIMMING ROUGH-CHISELED END

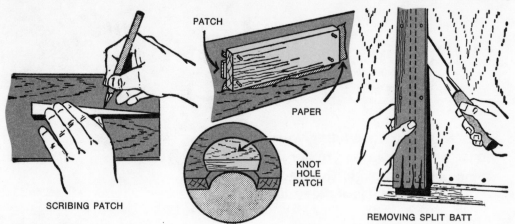

SCRIBING PATCH

PATCH

PAPER

KNOT HOLE PATCH

REMOVING SPLIT BATT

split, cut a wedge of wood larger than the crack and slightly thicker than the siding. Bevel the edges toward the back. Hold the patch in position over the fault, and trace around with a sharp pencil. Saw along the line with a compass saw, and then true and bevel the edges with a file. Coat all joining edges with resorcinol waterproof glue, and push the plug into place. Cover with a strip of paper, and clamp by temporarily tack-nailing a board over it. When the glue dries, remove the clamping board and plane the plug flush, filling any cracks with plastic wood. Sand, prime and paint.

Split batts over joints due to shrinkage in vertical boards may cause leaks. Pry off the faulty batt, remove any nails remaining in the boards and clean the edges beneath. Paint the edges and backs of the new batts before nailing in place.

Sometimes decorative extra wide siding boards such as redwood will shrink so much the rabbets lift entirely off the boards beneath. If removing and renailing is not enough to bring them together again, metal inserts are the answer. The boards are usually badly stained because water has leached black matter from the asphalted felt behind them. You can resurface without a lot of labor by renting a portable belt sander. Use the coarsest grit belt for roughing and finer belts for finishing. Take the first cuts across grain along window or

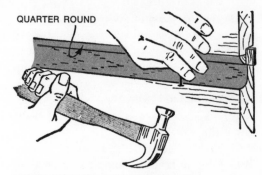

QUARTER ROUND

HIDING FLASHING WITH QUARTER ROUND

door trim. Then sand with grain until the main surface is cleaned. A small vibration sander is handy for touchup work around corners.

Close the rabbets with strips of sheet aluminum or galvanized iron. For easy handling, have your local tin shop shear them 3 feet long by ¾-inch wide. Slip these strips up into the rabbets of the boards and lap over the boards below, prying the upper boards out slightly with a chisel, if necessary. Drive the strips up with a strip of flat metal and hammer. If the strips tend to project outward, drive in brads. Then hide the metal with ⅜-inch quarter rounds primed with finishing material to match, and nailed into the lower edges of the siding.   E.M.L.

See also: CAULKING; HOME IMPROVEMENT; PAINT-ING, HOUSE; ROOFS; STUCCO.

How to Evaluate a Vacation Homesite

**The key factor in selecting
a vacation homesite—once you know you like
the general area—is water. Is potable,
drinking-quality water available,
and is the soil itself well enough drained to
allow use of a septic system for sewage?**

THERE IS NO QUESTION that an adequate supply of potable water is one of the most important factors in the total enjoyment of a vacation home. In a pinch, heating and lighting can be supplied by relatively simple means, but a house without water is simply unlivable. Therefore the time to start thinking about water is at the same time the property on which the house is to be built is being considered. For it is deep within the earth of this property that a safe supply of water can be expected to be found. Underground water, which has been filtered through many feet of earth and gravel and has been acted upon by earth bacteria and chemistry to remove today's contaminates, is virtually the only source of supply of satisfactory water for household use.

In considering property, the builder should be consulted regarding orientation and type of foundations and other factors. At this time it would be wise to call in a professional well driller, particularly one who has drilled previously in the immediate neighborhood. The Better Business Bureau is a good source of information on the reliability of various trades and services. The well driller will know within a reasonable doubt that water can be found, but he will not predict at what level. That can vary considerably within a small area. He will not quote a flat price, but will quote a figure based on the depth in feet he will eventually have to drill. He will also advise on the possibility of contamination from sources adjacent to the property such as farms or industrial plants.

A basic water system consists of a source (the well), the distribution system (piping and appliances), and the disposal of wastes (sewage).

The source. Water, in seeking its own level, seeps through the earth until it meets a strata of such density as to impede its progress. Thus it collects in subterranean pools, usually under pressure, so that when the pool is tapped by a well the water will flow freely into the void caused by the well. In drilling, a steel sleeve is inserted into the hole section by section to insure that the sides don't cave in. This sleeve, which extends the full length of the well, also prevents surface water at a relatively shallow level from entering the well to dilute the water at the deep source.

There is no such thing as an average well depth, but if satisfactory water is reached in the neighborhood of 30 feet or so, it is a fortunate economy. It could be many times that, and it is best to be philosophical about the cost of a deep well; good water is worth it.

When the eventual depth is reached, the driller will purge the well chemically and pump it temporarily for a period of time

site selection, mobile home: see mobile homes
skeet shooting: see shooting

to establish its reliability. When the chemicals have dissipated, a sample of the water is sent to the state water department for analysis.

As to volume, an average family today with modern appliances will use up to 1,000 gallons of water a week. The system should be capable of supplying no less than 500 gallons per hour. Thus the well must produce no less than 10 gallons per minute and preferably more.

If your lot is on a hill, check with neighbors above and below you for water problems. Rate of flow can vary considerably within a two acre area of lots.

Since the water will have to be brought to the surface and into the house; the advice of the well driller should be sought as to the type and capacity of the pump. A suction pump at the wellhead requires a well house to protect it, which could be unsightly. A pump within the house could be noisy. By far the most prevalent and practical pump in use today is the submersible. This is a self-contained impeller with electric motor in a water-tight casing which is lowered to the bottom of the well, and which jets the water up through a pipe into the house.

The system. When the water enters the house it is received in a tank so constructed that as the water rises a volume of air is compressed at the top of the tank. It is this pressure that will force the water through the house system with equal pressure at all outlets. The tank pressure regulator is interconnected with the submersible pump to form an automatic supply system.

The analysis from the state water department will show the bacterial content as well as the amount and type of suspended or dissolved salts and minerals in the water sample. If the latter is high, the department might recommend a filtering or purification treatment. This is a relatively simple appliance which can be bought or rented, and which is serviced every couple of weeks

by the addition of harmless chemicals or tablets according to the treatment required. The elimination or transformation of the salts or minerals which cause "hard" water will be immediately apparent in whiter washing and sparkling dishes and glassware. In some cases 75% of the soap action is used up to combat the hard factor, leaving only the remainder to do all the cleaning. In addition, the water contaminants will be deposited on the inside of pipes and boilers where they impede water pressure and eventually lead to serious damage and repairs costing many times that of the purifier.

Water supply piping for most residences is of flexible copper tubing with sweated fittings. Drain, waste, and vent systems are traditionally of cast iron and steel rigid pipe, but plastics are rapidly taking over in this field as well as in supply systems where local codes permit or have been revised. Venting the piping system, usually through the roof, is necessary due to the gas formed in the decomposition of wastes.

In planning a piping system it is advisable to remember an adequate number of garden hose outlets of the non-freezing type, and a hot-and-cold supply in the garage for car washing if you want one. Before landscaping, a spur out to a vegetable garden helps to eliminate extra long hoses. This branch should allow for draining in winter.

Regardless of other factors, such as pressure and volume, a successful supply of hot water will depend entirely on the capacity and speed of the water heating system. Once a 20 gallon tank was considered adequate, but today it should be 40 or even 50 gallons capacity. Hot water requirements in an average home can run to 60 or 70 gallons a day. A system that will raise the temperature of the incoming water to 150° F in an hour and maintain it there will be adequate. The heat can be supplied by electricity or gas, or the system

◄ *Most vacation home-sites are far from public water and sewage systems. This means that key factors in site selection are the availability of potable water and good enough drainage to permit the use of a septic tank and field.*

can be an auxilliary to the central heating furnace. Tanks should be well insulated, and the best ones are of stainless steel or glass lined. The local utility office is a good place to seek advice. It is important for comfort and safety that there be a high quality controlling device to prevent scalding temperatures at taps, tubs, or showers. There are special devices for controlling temperatures at shower heads, but in a good installation they should not be necessary. Appliances requiring temperatures higher than 150° such as dishwashers have built-in boosters. There are also devices which will supply instant boiling water (212°) at the kitchen sink for hot beverages.

Waste disposal. Most sections of the country now outlaw cesspools and seepage tanks, but a properly installed and maintained septic tank system is accepted in

➤ *Once your well is dug, you will have to decide on the type of pump you require. The three factors to consider are the depth of the well, the amount of water you will need and the amount of pressure required at the well to maintain a suitable pressure at the faucet.*

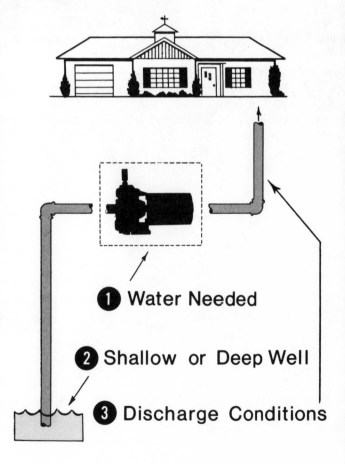

❶ Water Needed

❷ Shallow or Deep Well

❸ Discharge Conditions

almost all rural areas not serviced by community sewers. Such a system utilizes what is known as aerobic bacterial action which reduces household wastes in the tank to a watery effluent which is then allowed to seep through the ground for further earth bacterial action. The end result is water of a high degree of purity. The tank and the

seeping or leaching field is located at least 20 feet from the house, and downhill and on the opposite side from the well. The tank can be site-fabricated, or bought complete in welded steel or reinforced concrete. These latter have the advantage of correct design. The tank capacity should be 100 gallons for each member of the family; 500 to 600 gallons are average. The leaching field is commonly three parallel runs interconnected at the tank end, and extending in total to at least 35 feet; in clayey soil this should be extended half again. The pipe itself is loose jointed clay tile or perforated

▼ If you call in an expert to study the drainage of your property, he will probably dig some percolation test holes like the one shown here. These will indicate the rate at which the soil will absorb water.

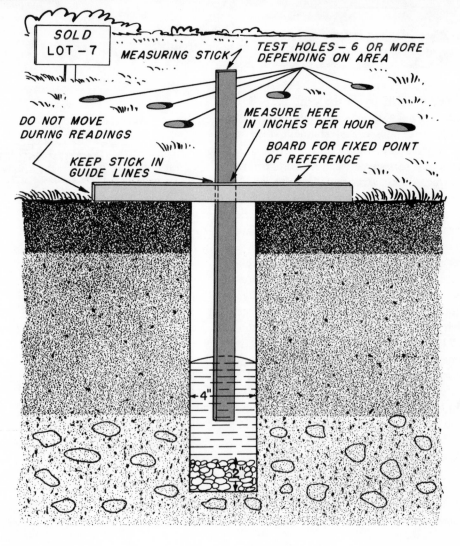

SOLD
LOT - 7

MEASURING STICK

TEST HOLES – 6 OR MORE
DEPENDING ON AREA

DO NOT MOVE
DURING READINGS

MEASURE HERE
IN INCHES PER HOUR

KEEP STICK IN
GUIDE LINES

BOARD FOR FIXED POINT
OF REFERENCE

4"

2"

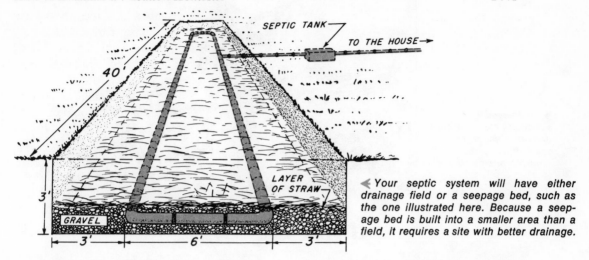

LAYER OF STRAW
GRAVEL

◄ *Your septic system will have either drainage field or a seepage bed, such as the one illustrated here. Because a seepage bed is built into a smaller area than a field, it requires a site with better drainage.*

bituminous fiber. The trench is about 30 inches deep with a generous bedding of loose gravel. Pipe is protected with a layer of straw, and the tank and field sodded over permanently. There is a manhole at the top of the tank which should be marked for access in an emergency, otherwise the system is good for five or more years with occasional commercially available stimulating treatments administered through the kitchen sink. In a new installation, the bacterial action is started artificially by the introduction of a commercial product, and thereafter it is self-sustaining.

The aerobic process requires the presence of oxygen, and grease inhibits this action and should be *strenuously avoided*. Otherwise a septic system is capable of handling the wastes from a grinding-type kitchen sink garbage disposal unit if the capacity of the tank is increased by 100 gallons. There is the possibility that the installation of a grease trap might be advantageous, and that question should be discussed with someone with industrial installation experience.

In short, the achievement of a successful water supply, distribution, and disposal system depends on the expert execution of three distinct trades or disciplines: well drilling, plumbing, and septic tank instal-

lation. The average homeowner will have to put a great deal of blind faith in those chosen to do this work. One form of insurance in selecting reliable performers is, as mentioned, checking their record with the Better Business Bureau. Another is a canvass of local opinions. There is much to be learned from casual chats with neighbors one is going to be living near, bearing in mind that these are not professional judgements. But a general consensus of reliability is hard to deny.

A fair percentage of local talent should be utilized in the various phases of home building, for it is reasonable to expect resentment if the major part of the homeowner's dollar is drained away from the community. On the other hand, there is the possibility of there being a chauvinistic attitude when local trades believe that in any case one or another of their number is bound to get the job and conspire to bid accordingly. These comments of seemingly irrelevance to the main subject of a sound water system are made to stress the importance of water in the overall picture of home-ownership, and that good water can be insured only by careful forethought, taking nothing for granted.

See also: HOME OWNERSHIP; MOBILE HOMES; NOISE; PLUMBING.

> Featherweight construction and squared ends combine to provide easily transportable and roomy sportsman's skiff.

Build a Lightweight Hunting and Fishing Skiff

You can construct this simple, easily transportable skiff in about two days at a moderate cost

I F YOU WANT A DEPENDABLE boat to poke around in rivers and marshes, this is the boat for you. And you can build it in about two days.

Its design was proven before the earliest settlers brought it to America. This, combined with modern simplified construction and lightweight materials gives you an extremely water-worthy boat. Add a 1-6 *hp* outboard motor and a car top carrier to this and you're free to go anywhere in search of fish, fowl and fun.

Start construction by laying out full-size drawings of the transom and stem on a plywood panel and cut them out. Cut the ¾-inch framepieces to length while they are clamped to the edges of the plywood parts. Lay out the notches for the chines, noting that the notches in the transom are cut through the frame only, while those in the stem pass through the plywood also. Cut the notches and then permanently fasten

the framing to the poorest side of the plywood with glue and 1-inch ringed asbestos siding nails. Space the nails 2 inches apart and slant them about 25° for maximum holding power.

Bevel the sides and bottom of the transom and stem, and attach the ¾-inch motor-board to the transom with 1-inch siding nails. Use an iron bar as a dolly to support the plywood while nailing and clinching exposed nail ends.

Assemble the mold frame from ¾-inch stock, using ordinary nails to allow the lumber to be salvaged when the mold frame is no longer needed. Connect the frame at the top with a ¾ x 1-inch crossbrace and add angle braces at each side to increase rigidity.

Cut a second plywood panel into three 16-inch widths. Lay out and cut the stern angle on two of these and cut the third width into two 4-foot lengths with the bow angle on each of these. Join the long and short sections with a ½-inch plywood batten to form the side planks. Join the sections at the centerline of the batten and glue with the upper edges flush, allowing 1⅝-inch on the lower edge to clear the chines. Fasten each batten with fourteen

Build a Lightweight Hunting and Fishing Skiff

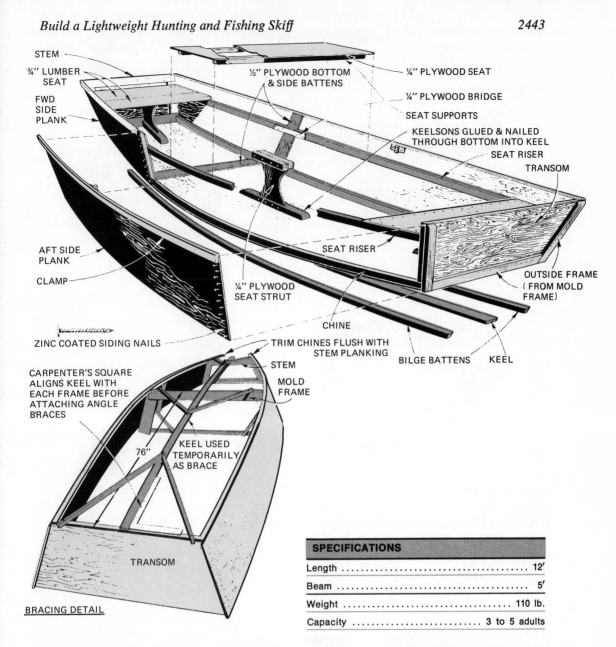

STEM

¾″ LUMBER SEAT

FWD SIDE PLANK

½″ PLYWOOD BOTTOM & SIDE BATTENS

¼″ PLYWOOD SEAT

¼″ PLYWOOD BRIDGE

SEAT SUPPORTS

KEELSONS GLUED & NAILED THROUGH BOTTOM INTO KEEL

SEAT RISER

TRANSOM

AFT SIDE PLANK

CLAMP

¼″ PLYWOOD SEAT STRUT

SEAT RISER

ZINC COATED SIDING NAILS

CHINE

TRIM CHINES FLUSH WITH STEM PLANKING

BILGE BATTENS

KEEL

OUTSIDE FRAME (FROM MOLD FRAME)

STEM

MOLD FRAME

CARPENTER'S SQUARE ALIGNS KEEL WITH EACH FRAME BEFORE ATTACHING ANGLE BRACES

76″

KEEL USED TEMPORARILY AS BRACE

TRANSOM

BRACING DETAIL

SPECIFICATIONS	
Length	12′
Beam	5′
Weight	110 lb.
Capacity	3 to 5 adults

#7 x 1-inch flat head wood screws, trimming the ends of the screws when the glue has dried, which takes about 12 hours at 80°F.

Have someone hold the transom in position while you temporarily nail on the side planks with two or three ordinary nails. Then locate and nail the mold frame in place in the same manner and nail the keel along the exact center of the transom, mold frame and stem. Have your helper hold the keel square with each frame while you attach angle braces to maintain proper alignment during construction.

Run a rope around the planks near each end of the hull, so you can remove the end frames without disturbing the rest of the assembly. Coat the mating surfaces of the

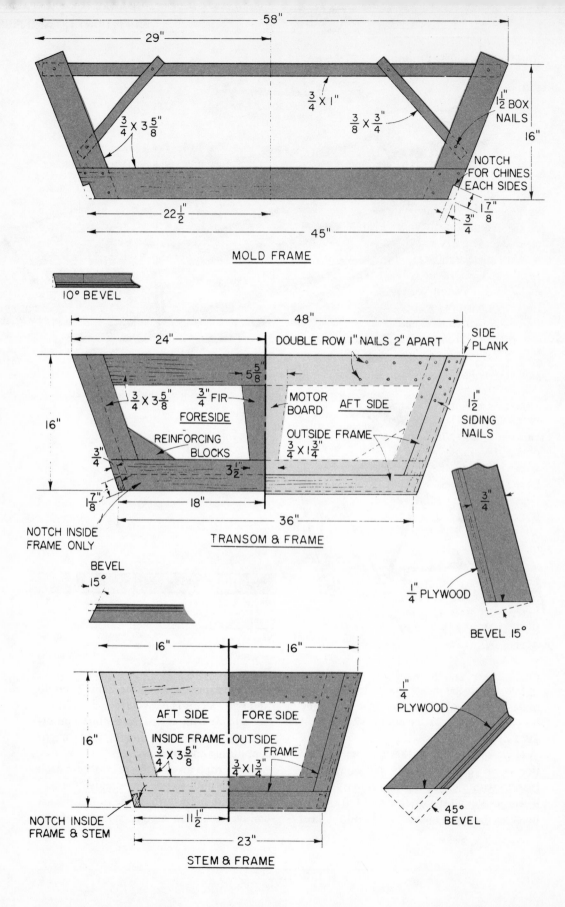

58"

29"

3/4 × 1"

3/8 × 3/4

1 1/2" BOX
NAILS

16"

3/4 × 3 5/8

NOTCH
FOR CHINES
EACH SIDES

22 1/2"

1 7/8"

3/4"

45"

MOLD FRAME

10° BEVEL

48"

24"

DOUBLE ROW 1" NAILS 2" APART

SIDE
PLANK

5 5/8"

3/4 × 3 5/8"

3/4" FIR

MOTOR
BOARD

AFT SIDE

1 1/2"
SIDING
NAILS

16"

FORESIDE

REINFORCING
BLOCKS

OUTSIDE FRAME
3/4 × 1 3/4"

3/4"

3/4"

1 7/8"

3 1/2"

NOTCH INSIDE
FRAME ONLY

18"

36"

1/4" PLYWOOD

TRANSOM & FRAME

BEVEL 15°

BEVEL
15°

1/4"
PLYWOOD

16"

16"

AFT SIDE

FORE SIDE

16"

INSIDE FRAME
3/4 × 3 5/8"

OUTSIDE
FRAME
3/4 × 1 3/4"

NOTCH INSIDE
FRAME & STEM

11 1/2"

45°
BEVEL

23"

STEM & FRAME

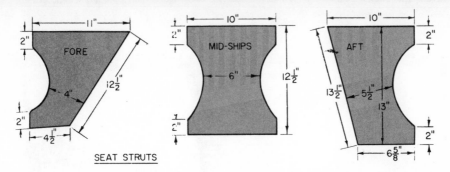

SEAT STRUTS

planks, chines and frames with sealer and insert 1-inch cloth strips coated with sealer in the plank joints. Now permanently assemble these parts with 1-inch nails.

With a straightedge, draw a centerline for the main bottom plank along the length of a third plywood panel. Divide this line into four 2-foot sections, drawing lines perpendicular to the centerline. Then mark the distance from the centerline at each 2-foot section as shown in the drawing. Drive nails partway at each of these points and bend a ¾-inch batten along the nails. Draw the outline of the plank along the batten and saw to shape.

Set the bottom plank in place on the chines, holding it with a few ordinary nails while checking the fit. If any adjustment is necessary, bend the hull to conform to the plank. Then caulk the joint between the bottom plank and the chines with sealer and cloth srtips, fastening the plank in place with 1¼-inch siding nails 1¼-inch apart. Use a double row of nails along the transom.

Glue and clamp a ½ x 4-inch wood batten from chine to chine along the inside front edge of the bottom plank. Fasten it with #7 x 1-inch flat head wood screws in a double row from the outside of the plank. Now attach the foreplank as you did the main bottom plank.

Temporarily nail the keel to the stem and transom. Then make the bilge battens by ripping a 12-foot 2 x 4 into three widths, approximately 1⅛-inch thick. Select the two most knot-free pieces and bevel their sides 15°. Round each end of these and temporarily nail the aft ends of the battens in place at the transom, 9 inches on each

side of the keel. While someone holds the battens in place, drill a ¼-inch hole 3 inches from the forward end of each. Now trace the outlines of the keel and battens on the bottom plank and remove them. Drill 1⁄16-inch lead holes at 1-foot intervals in the center of each outline on the bottom planks. Then replace the parts permanently with glue, installing the bolts and driving 2-inch siding nails at the transome and stem.

Now turn the hull over and support it on sawhorses. Draw lines through the lead holes and use them as a guide to drive 1¼-inch siding nails, 2-inches apart through the keel and battens. Use a staggered double row on the keel, spaced 1¼-inch on each side of center.

Rip a 1 x 4 in two lengthwise to make the sheer clamps. Rabbet one side of each ¼ x 1¼-inch and glue them to the top edges of the hull. Use 1-inch nails to fasten the clamps in place, spacing them 2 inches apart and clinching their ends on the outside of the clamp. Round the ends of the clamps at the transom and stem. Run a rope around the hull a few inches behind the mold frame, remove the frame and caulk the nail holes with wood filler.

Rip the seat risers with the saw blade set for a 22° bevel. Cut two lengths to fit from the after end of the side plank batten to the transom, and two more to fit from the forward edge of the batten to the stem. Bevel the ends of the risers to meet the frames. Glue and nail the risers from the outside with 1¼-inch siding nails, spaced 3 inches apart and bridge the side battens with a piece of ¼-inch plywood, attaching it as you did the risers. Attach seat risers to the

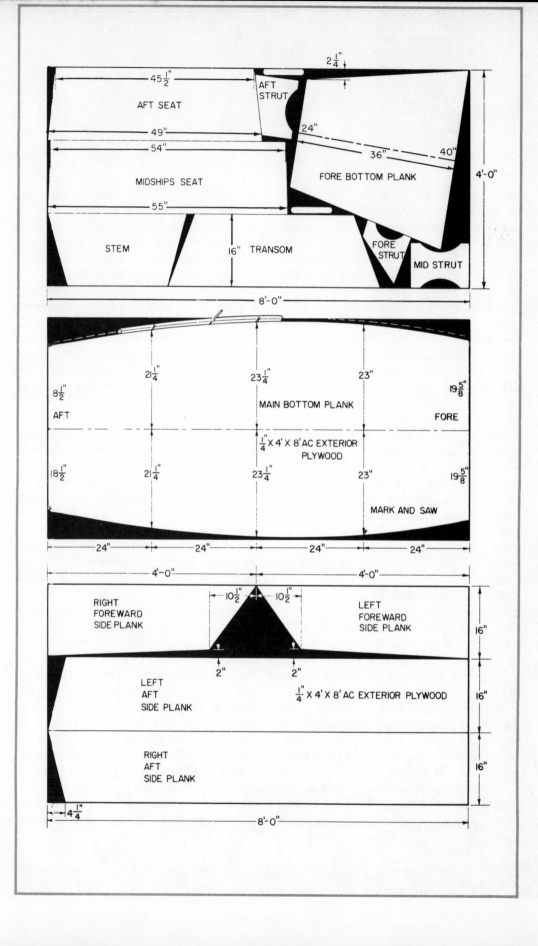

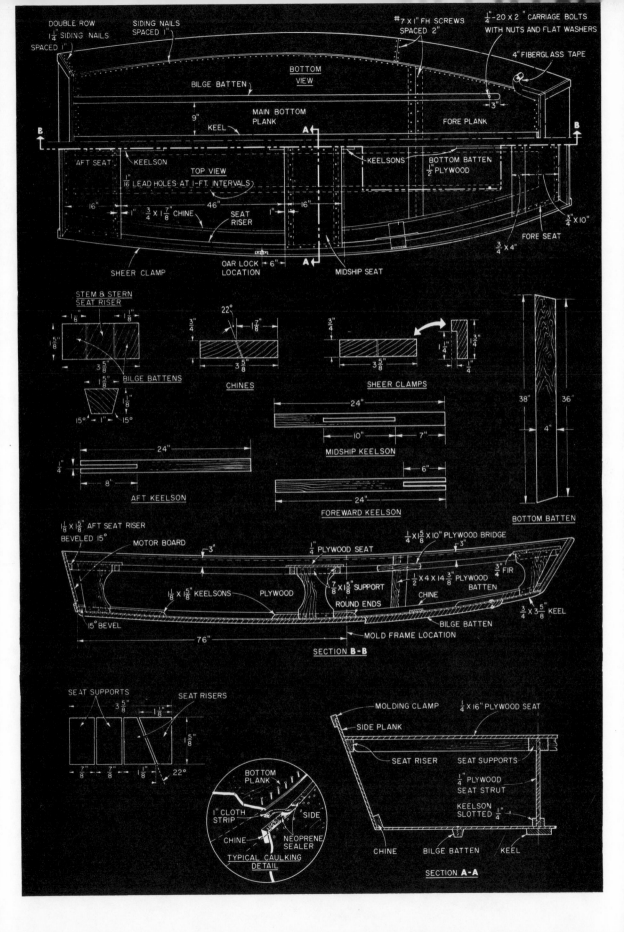

transom and stem, using 1⅛ x 1⅝-inch stock, beveled 15° for the transom and 45° for the stem.

Cut the aft and midship seat from the plywood panel and use a 10-inch and a 4-inch width of ¾-inch stock for the fore seat. Glue and nail 1⅛ x 1⅝-inch supports 1-inch from the edges of the midship and aft seats. Also attach supports to the top of the seat struts, cutting them to fit between the seat supports and the end risers. Cut the keelsons to length, round their ends as shown in the drawing, and cut ¼-inch slots in them. Glue and nail the struts into these slots.

Temporarily set the seats and struts in place, allowing 46 inches between the aft and midship seats. Mark the location of the struts on the underside of the seat and on the bottom plank. Then glue and nail the strut to the seat. Finish the assembly by nailing the seat boards to the risers and the struts to the bottom plank and keel. Use 1-inch siding nails for the seat assembly and 1½-inch nails when fastening the strut to the keel.

Salvage the ¾-inch lumber from the mold frame and rip each piece in half lengthwise to provide outside framing for the transom and stem. Caulk this seam with sealer and cloth and then nail with 1½-inch siding nails 2 inches apart.

Trim the excess glue from all joints and be sure the nail and screw heads are flush. Clinch any protruding nails and cover the exposed plywood edges with 4-inch fiberglass tape.

When dry, give the entire boat two coats of primer and one coat of your favorite marine enamel. Finally, install a pair of North River type oarlocks, 3 inches aft the midship seat edge and fit the boat with a pair of 6½ or 7-foot oars. Be sure to check with local authorities concerning small boat registration and required life-saving equipment.

See also: BOAT BUILDING; BOAT BUILDING PROJECTS; DUCK BOAT; FISHING; HUNTING.

MATERIALS LIST		
Quantity	**Size and Description**	**Purpose**
3	¼″ 4′x8′ AC fir exterior plywood	planking, seats, transom and stern
1	½″ 8″x40″ AC fir exterior plywood	side and bottom battens
1	¾″ 10″x6′ fir	fore seat and motor board
1	¾″ 4″x40″ fir	fore seat
2	¾″ 3⅝″x8′ fir	molding and stem frame
1	¾″ 3⅝″x10′ fir	transom frame
1	1⅝″ 3⅝″x12′ fir	seat supports
3	¾″ 3⅝″x12′ fir	chines, clamps and keel
1	1⅝″ 3⅝″x10′ fir	bilge battens and keelsons
1	¾″ 6″x9″ fir	motor board
as needed	#7 1″ flat head wood screws	
as needed	1″ zinc-dipped, ringed asbestos siding nails	

NOTE: Also need carriage bolts with nuts and flat washers, asbestos siding nails (1¼″, 1½″, 2″), glue powder, boat sealer, fiberglass tape and resin, oar locks and oars.

Jump the Bumps with a Single-runner Sled

This rugged, easy-to-build sled can give adults and children hours of fun in the snow

A FEW HOURS, SOME SCRAP LUMBER and 50 cents worth of hardware are all you need to fashion a single-runner sled for exciting winter sports.

No one knows for sure where the bump-jumper originated, but one thing's for certain—the bump-jumper is aptly named. For as it goes sailing along, its occupant guiding it by leaning his body from one side to the other, it occasionally hits a bump or dip in the snow. And when it does, it can leave the ground for 10 or 15 feet before alighting again. So, when fashioning your single-runner sled, try to keep balance in mind—it's important. And you'll assure yourself of a lot more winter fun.

The kind of wood you use doesn't really matter as long as it's sturdy and won't split or splinter easily. You can use pine, poplar or spruce, but if you want something heavier, oak or hickory will do nicely, too. And, of course, the seat can be best made from a piece of half-inch plywood. With the materials at hand and a few tools including a hammer, saw, drill and screwdriver, you can easily put together a professional-like single-runner sled within a matter of a few hours.

First, you'll need a piece of 2 x 6 lumber about 30 inches long, although you can make the runner either longer or shorter, depending on your own personal preference. Then, with marker and ruler, lay out the pattern of your runner making sure to provide considerable curvature at the front. Now you don't have to use a 2 x 6; a 2 x 4 will also work, but 2 x 6 is better and per-

2450

mits greater curvature to overcome obstacles in your path.

After you've laid out the pattern, saw out the runner. A bandsaw is best for this, although you can use a jig saw with a rip blade instead. This is the most difficult portion of the job because it's imperative that the runner has a flat bottom edge to insure proper balance.

▲ *The runner, about 30 inches long, is cut from a 2x6 and attached to a 2x4 post. A smooth 8x16-inch plywood board forms the seat, with small blocks of wood for handgrips.*

➤ *Four 3½x6½-inch pine braces secure the runner to the seat.*

Once the runner is fashioned, cut a piece of 2 x 4 approximately 8 inches long on the back side and an inch longer on the front. Make sure the cuts are even across because one end of this 2 x 4 you'll want to fit snugly against the top of the runner, the other firmly against the seat which must be level from side to side, but tilted to a slight degree backward. This will keep the rider from sliding forward on the seat of the device as he or she heads downhill.

To secure the 2 x 4 post to the runner, drill two or three evenly spaced holes through the runner from bottom to top midway from the front. Through these insert four-inch 12- or 14-gauge flat head wood screws. This is one of the greatest stress points on your single-runner sled. Once you've inserted the screws, you should finish the runner by placing a piece of strip metal 2 inches wide as a protective device to the wood. You may use broadhead nails for this (screw nails are best). But make sure to fit the metal against the wood snugly, pressing it firmly in place with your hand against the contour of the run-

ner. Six nails evenly spaced should be sufficient to hold the metal in place.

Your bump-jumper is now beginning to take form, but it'll need a seat. You can use a piece of smooth board 8 x 16-inch for best results. It should be at least ½-inch thick. Exterior plywood is suitable for such a seat and more sturdy than most wood of that thickness. Make sure to slightly bevel the edges to avoid cuts if someone should take a tumble and get hit in the head with the jumper on a downhill run.

Under the center of each end and parallel with that end, attach two ½-inch square blocks of wood just 4 inches long as handgrips. These can be secured to the underside of the seat with a heavy wood glue and reinforced with two 1-inch nails on each.

Placing the seat on top of the single 2 x 4 post, fasten it with two 9-gauge 1-inch wood screws. Next you need some bracing. Proper bracing is a most important ingredient in the anatomy of a bump-jumper. Cut four braces from 2 x 2-inch dressed pine lumber, each of them 3½ inches long on one side and 6½ inches on the other. In two of them, drill small holes at opposite angles on either end and place them fore and aft of the 2 x 4 post seat support, securing them with 2-inch wood screws.

Place the other two braces on either side of the 2 x 4 post, fastening them snugly against the bottom of the seat with screws from the top of the seat. Be sure to imbed the heads lest you find yourself with ripped pants and a red face at the bottom of the slope. In addition to the screws and nails use a good brand of heavy industrial wood glue. This is double protection against the braces working loose as you use your bump-jumper.

Now you're ready to do the finishing work. If you've used rough lumber, you'll need nothing more than a good coating of wood preservative. But if you've used dressed lumber, use a coating of wood preservative, then wait 24 hours before

⋀ *Finish with a good coating of wood preservative, and perhaps some wax or shellac, and you have a bump-jumper like this one.*

applying a coat of heavy duty outdoor shellac.

If you've used a piece of strip metal on the bottom of the runner, you likely will need to do nothing more to it, but if you've left the wood exposed, you might want to sand it well, then wax it with two or three coats, letting each dry in between. This will give the bump-jumper much more gliding power as you skim down the slopes, just as it would a set of skis.　　　　　B.T.

▲ *When stepping over logs or rocks, stand on top first and check the other side carefully. Snakes like to curl up under fallen logs, rocks, ledges and vegetation in wooded areas when the sun is out.*

Playing It Safe with Snakes

If you are trekking through snake country, you can protect yourself by wearing proper clothing and by staying alert

THE BEST DEFENSE against snakebite is to exercise extreme care when in snake country. If you must go where the snakes are, there is still a lot you can do to protect yourself.

First know where to watch for snakes and know how snakes behave, so you will know what to expect if you have the misfortune to confront one.

On camping trips, treat that log that you sit on, or that brush you walk through, or that rock you lift, as if there were a snake there. Use a long stick to probe ahead when you are walking through dense brush or anywhere you have doubts.

Rock hounds and climbers should be careful where they place their hands. Look before you grab.

Leather leggings over shoes, boots lined with fine wire mesh or heavy pants that may deflect the snake or cause him to misplace his strike can all improve your chances of survival. Thin shoes can be penetrated by the fangs of many snakes.

Wear high, leather boots over heavy wool socks when you're in snake country.

Playing It Safe with Snakes   *2453*

Loose-legged "engineer" style boots are preferable to laced models that fit snugly against the leg. Wear loose-legged, close-weave trousers outside your boots. In Florida, Texas and other warm states with heavy undergrowth, metal snake leggings are standard.

Build your camp in a clean area away from rocky ledges, brush or swamp, and sleep above ground, if you can. Some snakes like to stroll at night and might join you for warmth if the night is chilly. A rope placed on the ground around you will not turn them aside.

If you wade or swim, keep an eye out for swimming snakes, because they can strike and bite underwater and their bite is just as poisonous.

Poisonous snakes are most active and dangerous in the spring, when they come out fresh from hibernation with fully-charged poison glands. But treat them with respect at all times because it doesn't take much of their poison to make you very sick (even new-born snakes can give poisonous bites and dead snakes can bite by reflex action).

Do not let a fear of snakes keep you from enjoying the out-of-doors. Just keep your eyes open and take the proper precautions.

You may camp and hunt and fish for the rest of your life without ever seeing any sort of snake, but it is wise to learn to identify

▲ *Although poisonous snakes can bite from almost any position, they strike harder and farther (usually about 1/3 to 1/2 their length) from a coiled position.*

the poisonous ones and to know the effective methods of treating their bites.   J.R.

See also: CAMPING; FIRST AID; HIKING; PEST CONTROL; SURVIVAL; WILDLIFE.

POISONOUS SNAKES IN THE UNITED STATES			
Group	**Approx. No. Species**	**Average Length**	**Location and Habitat**
Rattlesnakes	11	5-7 ft. excl. rattle	Most of U.S., esp. SW. Plains, hills, wooded or rocky areas, often around farms
Pygmy or Ground Rattlesnakes	2	2 ft.	S, SE, Central States. Swamps, dry areas with low vegetation
Coral Snake	1	2½ ft.	SE, some in SW. Lowlands
Water Moccasin (Cottonmouth)	1	3-4 ft.	SE, some in Central States. In and around water
Copperhead Moccasin	1	2½-3 ft.	New Eng., Central States. Rugged country

> Southern Copperhead
Moccasin.

What to Do about Snakebite

The best way to deal with snakes is to avoid them. But, if you are bitten, you can avoid protracted, painful treatment or even death by using a snakebite kit or an anti-venom serum

O F THE APPROXIMATELY 2400 kinds of snakes that are known, about 60 are found in the United States. Only eight of these (divided into four major species) are considered dangerously poisonous: The coral snake, the copperhead (highland moccasin), the cottonmouth (water moccasin) and the rattlesnakes: Massasauga, pigmy, diamondback, timber and cane-brake.

Although the coloration and markings of the rattlers differ considerably, all of them have rattles on the end of the tail and the characteristic triangular head of the pit viper family, also common to the two poisonous moccasins.

The seven pit viper species (moccasins and rattlers) are also characterized by their two curved, hollow fangs, with which the toxic venom is injected.

The beautiful, but treacherous coral snake is a biter, rather than a striker, and prefers to chew on some member of its victim's anatomy to inject its highly dangerous venom.

Give all snakes a wide and respectful berth unless you are absolutely certain of their identity. In the mountainous southeast, the timber rattlesnake and the copperhead moccasin are the only dangerous species. In the areas where campers normally camp, they are seldom troublesome. Snakes don't like people and try to avoid them. You may have to do considerable looking to even see a snake near an established campground, but there are areas where rattlers and copperheads are fairly thick. The timber rattler, in the Alleghenies at least, prefers the high, wooded and rocky slopes of the mountains where he can get plenty of sunshine when he wants it and still be fairly close to food and his den.

In temperate climes, snakes hibernate to avoid the chill of winter. They become inactive at temperatures below about 40°F. When autumn approaches groups of snakes, often mixed groups of copperhead moccasins and timber rattlers, may be found near dens preparatory to their long winter of inactivity. Again, usually, in May, in the

➤ *Western Water Moccasin.*

➤ *Louisiana Milk Snake (not poisonous) and left, poisonous Texas Coral Snake.*

➤ *Massasauga Rattlesnake, also called Swamp Rattler.*

middle Atlantic states, they may be found in considerable numbers outside the dens. In the deep South and Southwest, snakes may remain active all year.

It is a fact that snakes seldom strike at targets more than half their length away; their most effective distance for accuracy and quick recoil. The maximum distance

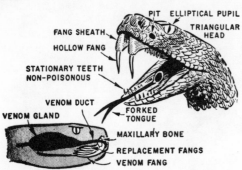

The hollow fang of the pit viper sits in a socket of the movable maxillary bone, with replacements ready to move into position when the fangs are shed (about once a month). When the mouth is closed, the fangs are folded against the roof; when the mouth is opened, they move forward and downward. The coral snake has short, fixed fangs.

is about three quarters of the snake's body length. If you encounter a snake at more than this distance, say six to eight feet, the safest defense is a quiet retreat. Don't stop to measure the snake or the distance. It will not chase you and, once it realizes that there is no danger to his own well being, it will usually move away.

Most experts agree that the American varieties of poisonous snakes will not chase you. Nor do they spit venom at you, though if their strike is short, some poison may be scattered on you. It won't harm you unless it gets into open cuts or your eyes, but wash it off immediately.

The serpents play an important part in nature's delicate balancing act and, in the wilderness at least, should be left to their own pursuits. Of course poisonous snakes must be eliminated when found near human habitation, recreation areas and similar places. However, the snakes usually take care of this themselves when premises are kept free of suitable hiding places: lumber piles, rocks, rubble, thick undergrowth or tall grasses.

Nevertheless some 6500 to 7000 careless humans are snake-bitten in the United States every year. Although the death rate is low because of ever increasing knowledge of the treatment of snakebite, the ordeal for the victims is a terribly painful experience, sometimes involving weeks or months of illness, amputation or other permanent handicaps.

A snakebite kit should be a part of every outdoorsman's personal equipment. There are several excellent ones on the market. They are available, complete with instructions from most drug stores. They could save your life.

Any individual who plans an excursion into snake country alone, and away from medical help, should consult his personal physician about the use of anti-venom. If administered within four hours after a snakebite has occurred, the serum is effective in reducing the dangers, discomforts and possible disabilities associated with snakebite.

Treatment of the snakebite victim must begin immediately after the injury. But treatment must be done with deliberate speed, not in panic. The victim should try to remain calm and not exert himself any more than is absolutely necessary.

The universal, medically approved first aid treatment for snakebite is the famil-

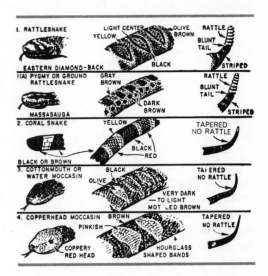

iar T. C. S. (Tourniquet-Cutting-Suction) method described in all first aid books and which accompanies all snakebite kits. Your chances of complete recovery with this method are excellent if you keep quiet, *don't* take anything alcoholic, and *do* apply a constriction band (tight enough to restrict flow in veins but *not* in arteries) about 2 inches above bite; loosen it for one minute every 15 minutes. Make small cuts at bite and on advancing edges of swelling (be careful not to sever a large blood vessel or tendon); apply suction at cuts for 15 minutes every hour with cups from a snake-bite kit or with your mouth (if you have no lip or mouth cuts). Inject antivenom if you have it; if you don't, try to reach a physician to do this within two hours after the bite.

Somewhat newer and less well known is the T. C. (Tourniquet-and-Cryotherapy) method much used in the southwestern United States.

The T. C. method prescribes the immediate use of a tight tourniquet, tight enough to nearly stop circulation, applied above the bite. The band must be loosened for one minute out of every ten.

The affected part is then immersed in a vessel of heavily iced water. When the limb is thoroughly chilled, the band or tourniquet is loosened and left loosened as long as the limb is kept immersed in the very cold water. Re-ice the water frequently. The limb may be kept in the cold solution for hours.

After an hour of icing, the limb may be removed from the water, dried and placed in a plastic bag before reimmersion in the ice-cold solution. This may be more comfortable for some victims. However, the bite itself should be kept damp to encourage leaking out of the venomous fluids.

Some doctors recommend the T. C. system as being the safer and simpler method for the layman to use. Since cutting is not involved, the risk of secondary bacterial infections is minimized, thus checking pain. The icing may be uncomfortable but the discomfort cannot compare with the full agony of actively spreading venom. The cold slows down the spread of the poison and allows the system to gradually absorb it.

An additional advantage of T. C. is that it allows time to reach medical aid and gives the doctor time to consider cutting, suction, serum tests, antitetanus and other procedures before antivenin treatment. Ice baths have been used for days with good results.

If medical aid is not available, the test for continued cold treatment is to discontinue the treatment for a short time. If the victim feels the action of venom near the bite and experiences sharp pains, continue the ice treatment.

Where ice is not available, good results have been obtained by using Freon or other aerosol refrigerant sprays. The freezing spray must not be used directly on the skin as it might cause frostbite. Instead spray a damp folded cloth, such as a handkerchief. The spray freezes the cloth and continued spraying, at intervals, keeps it frozen. Place the folded ice cloth directly over the bite, or wrap it closely around a bitten finger or toe.

Although the T. C. method has not won general acceptance, some medical men and T. C. S. advocates are now including ice packs or baths in their methods.

See also: CAMPING; FIRST AID; HIKING; WILDLIFE.

WHERE TO FIND IT

There are several snakebite kits on the market including those made by the Cutter Laboratories, 4th and Parker, Berkeley, Cal. 94710 and by Becton, Dickinson and Company, East Rutherford, N. J. 07073. They are available, complete with instructions, from most drug stores.

The North Carolina State Museum in Raleigh has published a most useful snake and snakebite booklet which includes full color illustrations of the principal poisonous snakes of America. Write to them for more information.

How to Remove Paints and Varnishes

Removal of the old finish is often the best way—sometimes the only way—to prepare a surface for refinishing

REMOVING A FINISH such as paint or varnish from plaster or wood is usually a more difficult job than applying it in the first place. But there are solvents that ease the work, and a good job of paint or varnish is essential for professional-looking results when refinishing is completed.

There are a variety of paint and varnish removers on the market. Some are flammable and others are not. Be sure to use a non-flammable type if there is any danger that the vapor can reach an exposed flame or when ventilation is poor.

In addition, some paint removers require no washing of the surface after the softened finish has been removed—these are general-purpose types and are often the easiest and least expensive to use. Other types do require washing, either with water or a solvent. Often, water-wash removers are best for epoxy, polyurethane and some water-base paints.

Removers that require a wash with a solvent usually contain a waxy substance that forms a film over the surface to keep the remover from evaporating before it does its work. After the paint sludge is scraped away, any trace of the waxy sub-

stance must be washed away with solvent. If left in place, it may keep any new coating from bonding well with the surface.

For large areas where ventilation is good, such as exterior walls or trim, a no-wash general-purpose remover is recommended.

Usually, the procedure for a no-wash remover is to apply it with the flat side of the brush, always stroking in the same direction and not working the brush back into areas that have just been covered.

Keep covered for about 20 minutes. Then, test the place where you started with a scraper. If the paint is softened down to the bare surface, begin scraping away the sludge. Use the broadest scraper practical.

If the paint is not softened down to the bare surface, apply a second coat of solvent over the first coat. Generally, two applications and a total of an hour's time will soften most paints. However, if there are many layers of paint, a third application of remover may be necessary.

No matter how many applications are required, be patient. Do not start scraping until the paint is softened all the way to the bare surface. Let the solvent do the work.

Trim and doors may be more difficult than walls because they are often painted more frequently. If possible, remove doors so they can be worked on flat.

Doors may have fancy molding or carving, where the paint is considerably thicker than on the flat portions of the surface. If this is the case proceed as you ordinarily

> Once the old finish has been thoroughly softened, use a fine wire brush to remove sludge from grooves and low spots on carved furniture or molding.

◄ A convenient way to remove softened paint from turnings, such as chair spindles, is to entwine steel wool on a string.

> Use steel wool wrapped around the tip of a lollypop stick to remove softened paint from crevices in carved wood.

would for any other paint removal job, but be satisfied with merely scraping out the heavy layers in the grooves of the molding. When the balance of the door is stripped, give the moldings an additional application of remover and when the final layers of paint in the grooves have softened, clean the grooves with a wire brush and coarse steel wool.

No-wash paint remover can also be used indoors. Use it the same way as you would for an exterior surface, but be sure to protect floors or other areas where you are working. One other word of warning. This type of remover will not soften calcimine, casein-based paint and some other water-based paints. Use water and washing powder to remove calcimine. Most other water-based paints can be softened with a water-wash type remover. Always consult your dealer and read the instructions on the container before purchasing any paint remover.

On plaster, apply the paint remover in the same way as on an exterior wall. Use a three-inch scraper. A narrower one will be more likely to gouge the surface.

Wash the stripped wall with a solution of water and washing powder, rinse it and fill all cracks. When the wall is completely dry, it is ready for a new coat of paint.

Removing paint from interior woodwork, kitchen cabinets and the like is somewhat more painstaking than exterior paint removal because greater care must be taken to protect other surfaces such as floors or adjacent areas where the paint is to be left on the surface.

Be sure to remove all hardware and cover electrical outlets with masking tape. If you have fancy moldings to contend with you will need a molding tool, or anything of suitable shape to scrape irregular surfaces. If need be, you can make scrapers specially adapted to your molding with a file and piece of sheet metal.

Coat only a small area at a time with paint remover. As soon as the paint is softened, scrape away the sludge. If you are going to repaint the stripped area, clean it up with steel wool.

If you are going to use a stain or a clear finish, apply an additional coat of remover and go over the surface with No. 2 steel wool. Also go over flat areas with a scraper to make sure all of the old finish has been removed. Then, rub the entire surface with dry steel wool and wait at least four hours before refinishing,

If you are refinishing furniture, the same general rules apply. Repair any loose joints, cracks or splinters before removing the finish. The old finish will protect the piece from glue stains as well as from damage that might occur while you are working on it.

Surface scratches, gouges and abrasions, of course, should be repaired after the piece has been stripped of its old finish.

Apply the remover to the piece as you would to any other work, painting it on with the flat side of the brush in one direction and not working the brush into areas that have just been covered. Test after twenty minutes. If the finish is softened down to the bare wood, start removing the sludge. If it isn't, recoat the piece with solvent, wait twenty minutes and try again .

In curved, grooved or irregular areas, use some steel wool on the end of a dowel or lollypop stick to remove the sludge. Also, a length of burlap can be used, especially on turnings, such as chair spindles and legs. For small grooves in turnings, entwine a length of steel wool with a piece of string. Another aid for irregularities in the surface is a fine steel brush.

When all the sludge has been scraped away, go over the work with medium-fine steel wool to remove any residue of softened paint. Allow the work to dry for at least four hours before refinishing.

You may find a water-wash type paint remover easier to use, although it may be more expensive. This type of paint and varnish remover is applied in the same way as no-wash remover. But, on most surfaces, the softened finish can be removed with a wash of cold water and scrubbing with a stiff brush or steel wool.

There are also specialized paint and varnish removers designed for use on the generally tougher finishes used on boats. They are used in about the same way as ordinary paint removers.

See also: FINISHING, WOOD; FLOORS; FURNITURE, USED; PAINTING; PAINTING, HOUSE; STAINING.

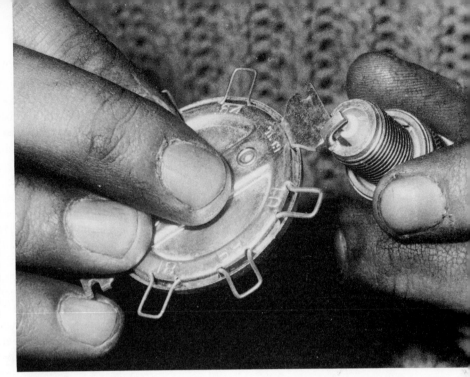

> *Regapping spark plugs. Only bend the side electrode. Always measure with a wire gauge. (A flat gauge gives a false reading in many cases.) Wire gauge fits in and is withdrawn with moderate drag.*

Trouble-shooting
Your Engine's Spark Plugs

The attention you give your car's spark plugs can improve its performance and, if you know how to read the signs, help you diagnose other engine problems

YOU CAN LEARN A LOT about a car by inspecting its spark plugs.

For example, the type of deposit on the firing end of the plug can reveal how the car has been operating.

If the deposit is wet, black and oily, the car probably pumps oil, due to worn rings, pistons or cylinder walls, or worn or sticky valves. Or the ignition system may not be supplying enough power to the plug.

The plug itself may be faulty—with a badly worn electrode, or even a cracked insulator. These, too, are clues to the condi-tion of the car, and to the type of service attention it has been receiving. Once you learn how to read such clues, you can usu-ally correct the trouble, and avoid some burdensome repair bills.

Before removing a spark plug for inspec-tion, carefully blow any dirt out of the spark plug well. This will keep dirt from falling into the combustion chamber when the plug is taken out. Pull the wires from the spark plug terminals *gently* until the snap fitting comes free. If you jerk them, you may separate the wire from the termi-nal connection, and although a broken lead wire isn't visible, it will form a secondary spark gap and eventually burn through the ignition cable, causing electrical failure.

Always pull by the spark plug wire's terminal, not by the wire itself. On to-day's cars with resistance wire, careless removal almost always results in internal damage to the wire, and the engine misfires.

2462

Trouble-shooting Your Engine's Spark Plugs

◄ All plugs normal. If all plugs have light tan or gray colored deposits and a small amount of electrode wear (not more than about .005-inch gap growth), plugs probably can be cleaned, regapped and reinstalled.

► All plugs fouled. These plugs may simply have been "drowned" with wet fuel during cranking. If choke is operating correctly, fouling may be engine oil. (Is car burning a lot of oil?) Fouling can be retarded by use of a hotter plug or a booster gap plug.

◄ One plug fouled. If only one plug in a set is carbon fouled and the others appear normal, check the corresponding ignition cable for continuity. A compression check or cylinder leak test might also indicate mechanical trouble in the one cylinder.

Trouble-shooting Your Engine's Spark Plugs

➤ One plug badly burned. If one plug in a set has melted electrodes, preignition was likely encountered in that cylinder. Check for intake manifold air leaks and possible crossfire. Be sure the one plug is not the wrong heat range.

◀ One or two plugs "splashed" fouled. Some plugs in a relatively new set may have splashed deposits. This may occur after a long-delayed tune-up when accumulated cylinder deposits are thrown against the plugs at high engine rpm. Clean and reinstall these plugs.

➤ Chipped insulator. If one or two plugs in a set have chipped insulator tips, severe detonation was likely cause. Bending center electrode during gapping can also crack insulator. Replace with new plugs of correct gap and heat range. Check for over-advanced timing.

As you remove the plugs, first check each gasket washer. The surfaces of the washer which contact the plug and cylinder head should be bright, clean, uniform and unbroken. And the washer itself should not be completely flattened.

If the gasket washer is discolored, corroded, or irregularly marked, the plug was not tightened enough during installation. This produces an incomplete seal which allows gases to leak by, and the plug to overheat. And such overheating will cause rapid wear of the electrodes and preignition.

On the other hand, an entirely flattened washer means that the plug was tightened too much, and this will often cause a fracture in the plug shell, stretched threads, or a cracked insulator.

Flash over. When an insulator has been cracked during installation and this crack fills up with a film of dirt and oil, you will have a condition known as "flash over." Electricity flows directly from the top terminal to the grounded plug shell, completely bypassing the electrodes and spark gap. The plug is thus short circuited, and the only remedy is to replace the plug.

You can also have a flash over condition when an accumulation of dirt and oil coats the top insulator enough to allow current to pass through it. The cure here is to wipe the insulator with a cloth moistened with a gasoline or alcohol solvent which will cut the oil film.

When flash over occurs at the upper insulator, it may be visible in the form of a dim blue spark discharge around the plugs. This is sometimes confused with corona—

the steady blue light that will appear around the base of the upper insulator, indicating a high tension field.

Inspecting the electrodes. Electrode inspection is your next step. Here you may encounter the examples of fouling or deposit accumulation, as mentioned earlier. If the electrodes are covered with a wet oily deposit, the plugs will probably give you good service after they have been cleaned and regapped. Such deposits are tell-tale signs of oil pumping in the engine, however, and you should check for worn valves or valve guides, rings, piston and cylinder walls. New rings might cut down the pumping. Or the battery or generator might be ailing to the point where not enough power is being delivered to the plug for proper ignition.

When the electrodes are coated with a hard, baked-on deposit, it's a sign that too cold a plug is being used in an oil-burning engine. You should change to a hotter plug. If such oil fouling then continues, you'll need an engine overhaul to correct the trouble at its source.

What is meant by cold or hot plugs? To function properly, a spark plug must operate within a specific temperature or heat range. So all plugs are classified by heat ranges as well as by size, thread and reach.

The heat range of a plug is primarily

> *Mechanical damage. A broken insulator and bent electrodes result from some foreign object falling into the combustion chamber. Because of valve overlap, objects can travel from one cylinder to another. Always clean out cylinders to prevent recurrence.*

➤ *All plugs overheated. When entire set has dead white insulators and badly eroded electrodes (more than .001-inch gap per 1000 miles), next colder heat range plug should be installed. Be sure ignition timing is not over-advanced.*

◄ *"Question mark" side electrodes. Improper use of pliers-type gap tools will bend the side electrode and push the center electrode into the insulator assembly. Because of the force multiplication exerted by these tools, use them with care.*

➤ *All plugs worn. If all plugs have tan or gray colored deposits and excessive electrode wear (about .008 to .010-inch more than original gap), they probably have over 10,000 miles. Replace entire set with new plugs of same heat range.*

controlled by internal exposed length of the center insulator, and is, basically, the speed with which the electrodes will cool after the cylinder fires. The electrodes must remain hot enough to prevent fouling, but must not get so hot that they will ignite the fuel mixture without an electrical spark (preignition).

The problem is that combustion chamber temperatures vary greatly with the type and condition of the engine, how fast it is run and the load it is pulling. For example, when an engine fitted with spark plugs of intermediate heat range is run at slow (city traffic) speeds for a long time, the electrodes will stay cool enough to allow deposits to form rapidly.

This electrode fouling causes the plugs to misfire, and you get hard starting, poor gas mileage and a loss of power. But when the same plugs are given a high-speed workout on the open road, many of the deposits may be burned away, in effect cleaning the plug. So, if you are getting spark plug miss from city driving, take your car out on the open highway and run it hard for an hour or so. Really run it up to peak engine speed and hold it there for a few seconds before you change gears. Such a "hard run" treatment may be the cheapest tune-up you can get.

It helps to clean away the type of fluffy dry carbon deposits in the electrode and inner insulator which are caused by gas-fouling. To prevent a recurrence of such rapid fouling, you might—in addition to regular high-speed workouts—lean down the fuel mixture by adjusting the carburetor. Then, if you still get rapid fouling, even after a carburetor adjustment, it might be wise to change to a hotter range of spark plug.

White, yellow, brown deposits. The most common form of deposit fouling results in white, yellow, brown or red coatings on the electrodes. These are normal by-products of combustion which result from the many additives in today's fuels and lubricants. In their original powdery form, they usually have little effect on spark plug operation. But when high speeds or heavy loads raise the engine temperature enough, such deposits melt and form a glaze coating on the inner insulator. When hot, this glaze is an excellent conductor, and allows the current to follow the glaze instead of jumping the spark gap.

Periodic sandblast cleaning usually removes these coatings and restores the plugs to proper operation. If the deposits are compacted between the plug shell and the inner insulator, however, replace the plug. It is almost impossible to remove such compacted deposits without damaging the insulator.

The sandblast treatment, available at some service stations, is the most effective way to clean the face of the plug and the inner insulator. It won't always remove all the scale and oxide deposits from the center electrode and from the underside of the ground electrode. So, to ensure clean firing surfaces, try bending the ground electrode up slightly and cleaning both surfaces thoroughly with a flat distributor-point file.

After a cleaning, you frequently discover other faults, such as a broken inner insulator. This may be caused by carelessness in regapping, or sustained operation with heavy detonation and preignition.

If the lower insulator is cracked and the center electrode worn to a fine point, while the ground electrode shows no sign of wear, the plug is operating too hot. The solution is to discard the damaged plug and replace it with one of a lower heat range.

Damaged plug shells are unusual. They are always the result of such mishandling as overtightening during installation. The damage generally shows up as a crack in the threads near the gasket seat, and such a plug should be promptly replaced.

Electrode wear. Once the fouling deposits have been cleaned off the electrodes,

Trouble-shooting Your Engine's Spark Plugs 2467

you can check them for wear. As a rough guide, remember that a set of spark plugs, properly cared for and regularly cleaned and regapped, should give you good service for about 12,000 miles. Considering that the spark plug must give off from 1,000 to 3,000 sparks per minute while operating in gas temperatures as high as 4,000° F.—and also withstand explosive pressures of up to 800 pounds/psi—this is a remarkable life expectancy.

These intense pressures and temperatures, when combined with the corrosive gases in the combustion chamber, gradually wear the electrodes down to the point where the gap can't be effectively reset. Replace such plugs. Deposits may become too embedded to clean. Replace plugs once a year or every 12,000 miles, whichever comes first.

When the plug is fairly new, and shows substantial wear, the trouble may be faulty installation, too lean a carburetor mixture, an over-advanced spark, dirty or damaged gasket seats, or a plug which has too hot a heat range.

Cleaning and regapping. A good rule of thumb for spark plug servicing is to remove, clean and regap plugs at least once every 5,000 miles.

> *This is a Champion Plug-Master wrench, ideal for those inaccessible V-8 plugs. Handle is curved, ratchet head has universal joint.*

Notice how Plug-Master wrench fits in without the need for disconnecting or pulling out anything.

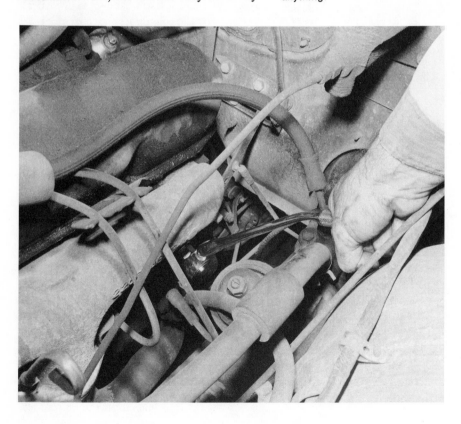

TO START THE FIRE

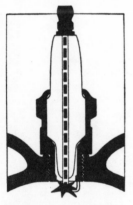

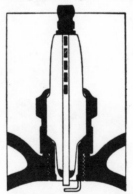

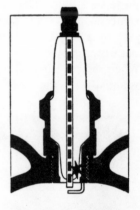

▼ SURFACE IGNITION

Sometimes a surface in the combustion chamber becomes hot enough to fire the fuel charge. Usually this type of ignition occurs before the timed spark and is called preignition. Deposits, overheated spark plugs, valves and sharp edges in the combustion chamber are all good sources of "hot spots." The driver may not be aware of the condition, but besides losing power, extensive engine damage could occur.

▲ NORMAL IGNITION

When a spark occurs at the proper instant across the spark plug gap, we can say that ignition is normal. This requires an ignition system properly timed, and delivering adequate voltage to plugs in good condition.

▲ TRACKING IGNITION

Instead of jumping the electrode gap, the spark may jump from one deposit "island" to another along the insulator nose. The fuel charge may be ignited, but the effect is to retard timing. Performance and economy are lost and the driver is unaware of the problem.

Always regap an old plug to the exact specifications set by the engine manufacturer. If you use a new plug, check it before installing to make sure it also meets the engine specifications. Make the gap adjustment by bending the ground electrode. If you bend the center electrode, you'll fracture the inner insulator tip.

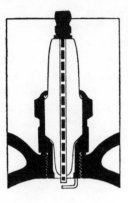

◄ *WIDE ELECTRODE GAP*
When spark plug electrode gaps become worn, the ignition system may not be able to supply enough voltage to jump the gap.

➤ *BRIDGED GAP*
If deposits bridge the electrode gap, coil voltage is shorted to ground. Under this condition no spark occurs to "start the fire."

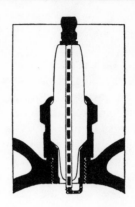

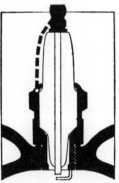

Misfire

▼ *FOULED PLUGS*
Some deposits that form on the insulator nose will conduct electricity. The coil, "seeing" this easier path to ground, will not build up enough voltage to jump the electrode gap.

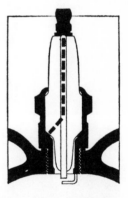

▲ *FLASH OVER*
When dirt, grease and moisture are allowed to accumulate on the spark plug insulator, high voltage may short over the outside of the insulator. Hard, brittle plug boots can encourage flash over. (Champion five-rib insulators help guard against flash over.)

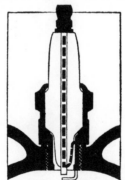

▲ *CRACKED INSULATOR*
A cracked insulator may allow high voltage to leak to ground. (Be careful not to damage the insulator with your gap tool.)

Always use a round wire gauge (from an automobile supply store) when setting the plug gap. Because the wearing away of the electrode tends to form a concave hollow on the underside, a flat feeler gauge cannot give an accurate gap measurement.

Seating the plug. The ideal way to ensure a correct seating of the plug is to use a

2470

torque wrench for tightening down the plugs. If you own one, and put in your own plugs, follow what the manufacturers recommend.

If you can't torque in your plugs, hand turn the plug in until it seats finger tight on the gasket. Then, using a proper fitting spark plug socket wrench, give it an additional half turn. This will produce the proper seal between the plug and the cylinder head.

When you go to buy a new set of plugs, remember that the manufacturer's chart

Trouble-shooting Your Engine's Spark Plugs

gives the recommendations for average driving (about 40% city and 60% highway). If you are on the highway a lot, covering most of your distance at fairly high-speed, you may need a plug that is a little cooler than average. If you're a "stop and go" driver, putting on most of your miles in the city at slow speeds with lots of waits at traffic lights, maybe a hotter plug will keep you going longer between tune-ups. P.W.

See also: IGNITION SYSTEM, AUTO; PARTS RE-PLACEMENT, ENGINE; TUNE-UP, ENGINE.